THE ANIMALS

THE ANIMALS

a memoir

CAROL HOULIHAN FLYNN

SADDLE ROAD PRESS

The Animals
© 2014 by Carol Houlihan Flynn

Saddle Road Press
Hilo, Hawai'i
http://saddleroadpress.com

Cover art by Patrick Flynn

Author photo by David Tarbet

ISBN 978-0-983307297
Library of Congress Control Number: 2014930014

v1.1

Dedicated with love to

David

Patrick and Molly

Emily and Andrew

Contents

Pig Heaven
11

The Pig Who Died
35

Collateral Damage
53

The Cat Who Bit My Foot
61

The Dog Who Was Deaf
91

How Much is That Doggie in the Window?
127

Dixie on my Mind
141

Roxie, Roxie, Burning Bright
153

My Last Dog
165

My First Dog
205

Ben Again
223

THE DEARNESS OF THINGS

From 1955 until 2002, I owned and lost eleven cats, five dogs, one guinea pig, two turtles, twenty-five newts and salamanders, two goats, two Brahmin Roosters, one Brahmin hen, one Rhode Island Red hen, sixty-seven temporarily-adopted, newly-hatched chickens, one Long Island duck, twelve Mallard ducks, six Peking ducks, and too many rabbits.

And I owned pigs. So many pigs—twenty-eight all told. One Yorkshire boar, one Spotted China sow, one Hampshire sow, their twenty-four children, and an orphaned Yorkshire gilt named Snowflake.

This is the story of these animals, an account of their lives, and an accounting of the dearness of things, an economic study of love and loss. For the animals are all, every one of them, down even to the smallest newt, born out of our desire for love. And that is where the problem lies.

PIG HEAVEN

OF ALL THE PIGS, SISSY WAS THE MOST OBLIGING. When we brought her home from Hogs and Logs that Saturday in the Poconos, that summer of 1981, she settled into her burlap sack and fell asleep between my feet. Meanwhile Jessie was snorting and biting and pissing and scratching. By the time we pulled into the driveway she had managed to root through her sack, and was beginning to eat the car mat. But then Jessie was another kind of pig altogether.

Sissy was a Spotted Poland China and, from the start, she looked like a child's idea of a pig. When she stood very still she looked like a piggy bank. Even at her grossest moments of pregnancy, when she was swollen with her ungrateful children, she seemed frail, almost brittle, as if she would break if she were squeezed too hard.

In spite of her apparent delicacy, she proved sturdy, and took a lot of abuse from Jessie, who was always a mean, snapping pig, and from Wilbur, who was always trying to mount her, even when she weighed thirty pounds to his seven or eight hundred. I used to worry that he'd break her back in two. She learned to ease into Wilbur's pelvis, and to lie very still until he stopped grunting and never to try to bite him the way Jessie would. In her way, she was appreciated for her virtues, her readiness to serve, and her ability to forgive. Most nights she ended up sleeping between them, creating a safe zone with her compliant body.

That first summer, we played at pig farming with an earnest, solemn fascination. We were four: Patrick, almost twelve, Molly nine, Denny, my husband, and me. Denny came for the weekends, from his job in the World Trade Center, but the kids and I stayed on all summer, the summer I planned to write and publish enough to get tenure at New York University. I was free the entire summer to write my book on the body in Swift and Defoe, but even freer to play with the pigs. Hardly a fair choice when everything fed my hunger for their sweaty, sweet substantiality.

Swift would have understood, I told myself, as we tried to build our first outbuilding, a shack tacked onto the garage. The pigs helped, turning the dog run filled with tall rank weeds and rocks into their mud hole: Wilbur lumbering, Jessie and Sissy scampering. All three rooted out boulders and consumed every living thing inside the hot wire fence. We sprayed water onto hard-caked topsoil, watching it turn into mud the consistency of manure. Choked streams formed shining black pools while fragile rainbows glistened in the spray.

We woke to the plaintive clucking of the chickens as they began to construct their daily case against the inept rooster, a magnificent Brahmin named Alexander who bounced occasionally against their tight resilient bodies. He seldom crowed and when he did was usually mistaken. Beneath the chickens' murmuring, the pigs made guttural snorting noises. They were still sleeping, dreaming of Bob the hired man, a genius who brought daily tributes of stale donuts and slightly spoiled yogurt, blackened bananas and split watermelons, moldy processed cheese and sterilized pig feed that cost $29 a bag. The pigs grunted in unison when he approached them carrying his heaving pail.

How they loved what he brought them. In the beginning, we loved to see their greediness—appetite in motion. When Wilbur cracked open the peach stones and drank down cartons of out-of-date yogurt, he made the gilts, Sissy and Jessie, look winsome and demure, even as they gobbled up cartons of large curd cottage cheese.

Patrick and Molly would spend long afternoons singing to them, pigs and kids stretched out in the mud, flicking away dull witted flies. Wilbur was large but tractable, most responsive to belly scratching and ear twigging. Molly could reduce him to rapture by energetically massaging the dry, silky membrane between his tender, hairy ears and his thick, bony skull.

That first summer I spent a lot of time in the pig yard scratching assorted ears and snouts. Sometimes I fed the pigs over-ripe peaches just to hear them crunch the pits between their grinning jaws. As the sun baked my brain and dried out the mud hole, I could feel myself dissolving, becoming part of the yard itself, part of the pigs themselves, their bodies stretched out against the shed.

But the pigs were usually in motion, rooting for bugs and excavating boulders. They liked to roll them around the mud hole. They also spent a considerable amount of time scratching their tough hairy backsides against the garage shingles. Even in their sleep, they would rotate their ears and twitch away curious flies with their wrinkled snouts.

I became particularly fond of those snouts, flexible and soft to the touch, moist and tender as fresh cut melon. Pigs explore with these elephantine devices, tentatively thrusting them forward to sniff out an offered hand, or more confidently burrowing them into fresh dirt in search of a smooth round rock to chew over. In an occasional frenzy they would work together, snouts uniting to unearth gigantic treasures like flagstone foundations long buried, mysterious pieces of concrete, boulders three or four feet across, and rusting pieces of a discarded tractor. After their efforts, they would flop down into their mud hole and grunt for more water.

When I remember those early days it is always three o'clock in the afternoon, the sun is high and bright and I am drinking something cold. I lean against the apple tree, feeling bark against my back. All I want to do is listen to the scratchy jangle of crickets hidden in the grass and breathe in the pig sweat and mud and manure and the sweet smell of fermenting corn.

I pretend to read Daniel Defoe, but I'm really attending to Wilbur. He's never silent, not even in his sleep. He snores gently, exhaling through his quivering snout. He must be dreaming of open fields and freedom, for he runs fast, his eyes shut tight, his little trotters briskly thrusting away from his solid flesh. He soars effortlessly over the hot wire to land in a field full of apples, and now he smacks his quivering lips and crunches down on a phantom red delicious. Awake, rooting, he makes new snorting noises as he attacks those rocks stubborn enough to resist him. Sometimes he sniffs amorously as if he were nuzzling Sissy.

Sissy shuffles aimlessly back and forth, mainly staying out of Jessie's way. Her voice is low, easy to distinguish from Jessie's strident snort. Both gilts squeal flirtatiously when they're sprayed, Jessie most loudly, demanding more and more water. Wilbur stares intently at the new-formed rainbow shining in the mud.

Of course, things changed when the gilts turned into pregnant sows. They gained at least two hundred and fifty pounds. But Sissy retained her delicacy. Her new bulk seemed inappropriate, emphasizing her fragility all the more. She carried herself tentatively, as if she were embarrassed to be taking up so much room. Fat suited Jessie, fortifying her in the daily battles she waged against her condition. Malcontent, ornery, she glared through her flashing piggy eyes. "What. A. Dump." we imagined her saying. Bette Davis at her bitchiest.

It was cold now, and the mud hole had frozen over, tempting the three pigs to slide across the ice, occasionally slamming into the garage wall. Jessie breathed out steam and grinned up at the gray skies filled with snow while Sissy huddled against the shed. She never could get warm enough. Doc said that she would toughen up, but he didn't say how. There were mysteries here that constantly escaped us. We had made a mistake mating the sows to farrow in the winter, he said. We had to watch them carefully. Bob assured us that he'd be able to tell when they were due. Trust me, he smiled, you know me.

We did, and that worried me. Hired man and rural entrepreneur, Bob ran our makeshift pig operation by the seat of his patched-over pants. Now that summer had ended, and we were only in the country on the weekends, we depended more than ever on his care.

And so, one Saturday morning in early December we found Sissy stretched out in dazed and mild astonishment as far away as possible from her dead children. Five little corpses, no child's idea of a pig here, lay face down in a small puddle. We never knew if they were born dead or simply drowned sometime in the night. One other piglet survived, a

16

tiny Yorkshire sleeping fitfully alongside Sissy's flank. We named her Emma. She looked just like Wilbur, and at first she kept falling off Sissy's teats, too many teats for one small pig. We had to teach her how to nurse.

Around this time Jessie dropped her first litter. The farrowing took less than an hour. Eight piglets, each one a Hampshire, each one a sturdy and self-reliant version of Jessie, were suddenly rooting furiously around the pig yard, butting and snorting as they chased the Brahmin hen. Occasionally they would rush upon Jessie's indifferent luxuriant body, and she would grudgingly allow them to suck. They all thrived, each one sleek and fat and mean. Sissy's one pig continued to scramble all over her mother, growing puny under her careful management.

Sissy was soon pregnant again. She had grown some, and the boar looked less monstrous now in his mating posture. Confronting her shining, muscled backside, he would sometimes lose his balance as he raised himself up on two trotters so precariously to enter into Sissy's ever-receptive womb. I would watch him carefully then, on the lookout for his prick. Boars are supposed to possess minuscule penises curled into a corkscrew shape the size of a pencil. This miraculous organ is invisible, tucked in between two swaying balls the size of muskmelons. His prick always eluded me, but my kids caught sight of it one hot summer afternoon. They were lolling around the pig yard, scratching Sissy behind the ears, when Wilbur rolled over in his sleep. They swear that he smiled and grunted, stiffened all over, and extended for approximately one minute his delicate instrument. (Boars can ejaculate for up to six minutes.) After he squirted his sperm into the heavy, loamy air, he settled down once more into the mud. I like to think that he was dreaming of Sissy.

Sissy farrowed again in the summer. This time Bob and I stayed up all through the night slapping away mosquitoes. I drank Jack Daniels while Bob remembered how he used to drink Jack Daniels. Patrick and Molly sat very still, waiting along with us for the piglets to emerge. We didn't talk much. They were a long time coming, but this time only one, a Spotted Poland China, was born dead. The umbilical

17

cord was wrapped around its stubby neck. Since Sissy didn't seem to know how to push down, sometimes we needed to reach inside her to pull a piglet out. I was surprised how easy it was to enter into her wet and trembling womb. After each birth, she would shudder, bury her snout into the hay, and fall asleep for forty or fifty minutes. Then she would shake herself awake to start all over again.

We were flying high that night. Denny brought friends from New York into the pen to admire the piglets. Bob taught us how to pull away the silky, slithery caul from the tiny, warm bodies, and how to cut the umbilical cord, while he clipped their miniature tusks with a sharp tool that vaguely resembled a guillotine. They didn't seem to feel pain, but newborn piglets are remarkably tough. Their eyes open at birth, their legs carry them sturdily across the shed floor, and their snouts instinctively root through the sawdust in search of smooth, round rocks to chew on. They quickly wiggled onto their mother's taut straining teats, and sucked noisily through the buzzing night, drowning out the crickets. Patrick and Molly finally fell asleep at three in the morning, their faces shining in the glow of the heat lamp.

We were triumphant that night, but also worried, for by now we realized that piglets grew at an alarming rate. It was not difficult to imagine the strain that eight more animals would place on our inadequate physical plant. The summer before, we had watched with astonished delight as Sissy and Jessie grew. Each day they seemed to nudge and root a little more towards the platonic form of Sow. We plotted their progress with pride, unable to see any problems with their development. Their differences, Sissy's abject sweetness and Jessie's meanness, only gave them more character.

When I look back on the photographs of that idyllic time, I cannot find one picture without a pig somewhere—growing. The snap shots of our second summer are fewer in number and relatively empty of pigs, full grown or new born. We had no more room for fantasies that turned too quickly into solid, stubborn flesh.

It was our fault from the very beginning. The fact was, we entered the pig business almost accidentally. One day, after cutting the grass, Bob started talking about his three-year-old boar. Wilbur (he wasn't Wilbur then, merely "the boar") had been living over at Bob's brother-in-law's farm, but Bob and his brother-in-law had been quarreling over Bob's work habits and the general decline of western civilization in northeastern Pennsylvania. Somewhere in this disagreement, Wilbur's virility was impugned. Consequently, Bob was looking for a place to raise his seven hundred pound boar, a paragon, he swore, not only potent, but also extremely polite.

We had known Bob for over a year. He started out cutting the grass, then shoveling the drive and generally "watching" the place when we were back in Brooklyn. He was particularly emphatic about our need for security and produced weekly reports of lurid, kinky break-ins inflicted upon weekend households that were left to their own devices. Now a pig, he argued, a pig on the property was the most effective burglar alarm the country could provide. Who would be so bold, so downright dumb, as to tangle with a seven hundred pound boar?

That's also why we had the chickens and the ducks and the rooster. They too were guaranteed to scare away criminals, a class notable for its timidity in the face of nature. Criminals were inevitably urban, pouring out of New York and Newark to ravage the innocent countryside. Only the animals could save us from these relentless assaults on our home.

We didn't believe any of this, of course, but we did accept Bob's animal offerings. They were initially free—Roberta, the neurotic Long Island duck, Henrietta, the Rhode Island Red hen, the twelve mallards, the six Peking ducks, the countless boring rabbits. (We paid for Daisy and Lily, the two timid goats.) But the animals did need to be fed and watered and "watched," tasks Bob diligently carried out. In spite of the frailty of Bob's many cars (each one breaking down in a new and unexpected way), in spite of his own erratic health, and in spite of the worst snowstorms in history, he would faithfully trudge through drifts shoulder-high to feed our animals.

By the time we got Wilbur, we were already animal poor. We had turned the garage into a barn reeking with the smell of sawdust and grain and hay and chicken shit. Growers' Feed Store down the road, where we stocked up on corn and rabbit pellets, and an occasional chicken, became the fixed point in our expanding household. I bought Alexander, the Brahmin rooster there—so pompous, imperial, and bristling—and Cleopatra, his modest, dumpy consort. She always seemed to be laughing at her master's unsuccessful attempts to mount her.

And somehow, around a particularly cold Easter, I ended up tending sixty-seven newly hatched chickens from Growers' because somebody's incubator had broken down. We had a special thermostat in the plant room, making it possible to provide torrid, steamy heat in the coldest weather, just what the baby chicks cried for. They also craved my plants and, peeping madly, scurried back and forth from plant to plant, diving, lunging, biting, destroying, pausing only to shit all over the red brick floor.

In the country, we kept testing the limits. Sometimes this worked. Molly had always begged for a dog or a cat, something that was hers alone. But we worried about her allergies. Dogs usually made her break out into eczema or start wheezing. She decided to make an experiment, and took a job down at Growers' Feed Store. She was responsible for the welfare of the kittens and puppies that folks left to be given away. It was her job to feed them and hug them and rub her face into their bodies. She insisted that they didn't make her sick. Look she would crow—no wheezing, no eczema. And she took her experiment even further, aided by Bob and his own love of animals.

For Molly had fallen in love with one of the puppies, a cross between a Pomeranian and a Cocker Spaniel that looked like a baby fox. We worried about keeping the dog full time, but decided to try her out on a part-time basis. Bob would care for Rosebud (soon known as Rosie) during the week and hand her over to us on the weekends. On her visits, we'd be able to test Molly's reactions to her fur and dander. And so, for several months, every Friday and Saturday night, Rosie would sleep curled up in Molly's arms and lick her awake in the morning, and never, not even once, did Molly sneeze or itch. It was time, we announced, to bring Rosie back with us to Brooklyn.

Then reality broke in. Molly might have been ready to live full time with Rosie, but Bob could never part with her. Rosie was his dog, his and Aggie's. Rosie needed to live in Newfoundland during the week. Always. Whatever would she do with herself in Brooklyn, New York? City life with its dirt and its crime and its traffic would drive her crazy. She was used to chasing the chickens and ducks and she would miss staring at Wilbur.

But the clincher here was Aggie. Rosie was her dog. She had earned that dog all right, taking extra special care of her. She was the one who fed Rosie all of her doggie treats.

"You'll just break Aggie's heart into little bitty pieces," Bob swore, "if you take her little bitty dog away from her." Why, Aggie had suffered Second Degree burns on her legs all because of little Rosie. Didn't we remember what happened when she was bending over the stove cooking up pots of gizzards to tempt the little dog's appetite? Rosie got under her feet and made her lose her balance. Didn't we remember how Aggie fell onto the boiling cauldron of innards, how it spilled all over onto her stomach and thighs? How could we take Rosie from her after those skin grafts?

And so Rosie stayed in Newfoundland during the week, and spent weekends in Molly's bed. Woe be unto us if we missed a weekend in the country. Rosie was waiting for us. If we didn't show up we'd break her little bitty heart in two.

But Bob was better than we were at rationalizing his animal greed. He procured so many animals for us because he loved them and wanted them to be cared for. We shared his greed, but we were less likely to sentimentalize it. We thought that Nature was there to be plundered. It was ours for the taking. Day Lilies cried out to be picked, rhubarb dreamed of being cooked into slimy concoctions that nobody would eat, while bull rushes waved expectantly from the swamp, offering their slender bodies up to us for our pleasure.

We wondered how the wild birds had survived before we started feeding them thistles and corn. Even the overweight raccoon owed much of his bulk to our involuntary contributions that he stole in the night. Had it not been for us, he would have wasted away. Without realizing it, we had become animal capitalists, raping the landscape because we could, because somehow it was the better for our taking care of it.

Our own domesticated animals depended upon us even more. Every last one looked to us for salvation, and we felt all the safer saving them. Their noises comforted me, particularly in the night when I would creep out to the pig yard to listen to Wilbur snore, craving the sweet subtle sound of animal breath inhaled and exhaled.

I would return then to our house, so substantial seeming, blazing against the darkness. But first I would sit against the apple tree and stare into the windows to catch a glimpse of my family. I could see Denny leaning forward, dwarfing the wing back chair. He'd be clutching a glass of Maker's Mark. Something would be playing on the T.V.—a documentary on World II or a catastrophic movie like "Escape From New York." Or maybe "Mad Max"—they loved Mel Gibson. The kids would be at Denny's feet playing "Battleship" while they watched New York City go up in smoke. Their blonde hair gleamed in the firelight. It all looked so snug and cozy. But it also looked scary, like an insurance ad reminding us that we are never safe.

I would look for constellations, for there were stars then, with no city lights to dim them, millions of stars so cold and remote, reminding me of my cosmic insignificance. I must have sat under the apple tree at least four hundred and twenty five nights those three years in the country. Sometimes I worried about the kids, sometimes I thought about the most recent fight with Denny. I thought about Cambodia, and Jim Jones, and, of course, I worried about getting tenure. The stars whirled overhead, propelling us all into some new, disastrous state. But then I would find myself filled with joy, rare and pure, a joy that most often came from the animals.

I needed those solid creatures of my imagination that I had tried to name and to set free. I needed them, but they didn't really need me.

At first they all had names. Those early days we marched forth with confidence, shaping the wilderness in our image. Wilbur even had a literary pedigree (its coyness still embarrasses me). While my friend Ann has never forgiven me for Jessie, bearer of one of her middle names, I am happy that we chose a tough name that suited such a strong, independent animal. Sissy's name was the simplest, fitting her sweet humility, lacking the grandiosity and pomposity of Henrietta, Alexander or Cleopatra, our Rhode Island Red and the Brahmins. We called Sissy's first gilt Emma, and made up names for Jessie's entire litter.

But it was very difficult to keep seven new pigs straight, and by the time Sissy's second litter came, we gave up altogether. Her children grew into nameless savages, restless and ill bred. Towards the end they would break down their hot wire en masse to trample the day lilies and root up the rhubarb, in search, perhaps, of an identity that had been denied them. Their greediness made me angry, but it also made me ashamed. It demanded rudely that we recognize how bad things had become.

We hadn't planned it this way. All the while we set up our original pig farm, we carefully avoided looking too far into a future of sexuality and death. It is, I am still certain, perfectly possible for pigs to become pets, but only under controlled circumstances. Gilts could no doubt live platonically, perhaps even happily, with barrows, castrated males, for a good many years, as long as they didn't develop arthritis. Barrows and boars could also most likely survive each other's company, perhaps even forming homosocial attachments. Before buying the gilts, we had actually considered introducing a barrow into Wilbur's pig yard. Bob protested, insisting that Wilbur would kill another male, but now I realize that Bob had his own agenda. He needed gilts, not barrows, if he were to demonstrate Wilbur's potency to silence his brother-in-law. But then we all projected onto the animals our own desires and needs.

That is why we decided that it would be unfair to deny Wilbur a fatherhood that he never once seemed to recognize. What he did experience in his paternity was isolation. Once his children were old enough to farrow, they needed to be protected from his desire for his virgin daughters, and from the rivalry that festered between him and the barrows, his castrated sons. I can still hear him squealing and moaning in lonely splendor, can still see him pacing back and forth, locked away from Jessie and Sissy and his twenty-four children.

We also reasoned that it would be needlessly cruel to prevent the gilts from farrowing. As caretakers of their porcine hormones, we were responsible for their right to reproduce. Unfertilized they would languish unloved. It is not entirely clear to me now exactly why their motherhood seemed so desirable. I was 35 years old then, and deciding with some ambivalence that I would have no more children, so possibly my own fears of curtailed maternity entered into this specious animal psychologizing.

I'm not sure what Denny was thinking when "we" made up our rules for raising the perfect pregnant pig. Maybe he was just going along with me, as frightened of me as I was of him. We appeased each other then with our plans, filling up the days in the country with jobs carefully crossed off the "to do" list, jobs—however outlandish—that promised to give our unraveling marriage purpose. We didn't count on the theoretical animals themselves growing so quickly into a substantial mass of flesh and blood, appetite and desire.

Our theories about the pig's sexuality became even more complicated by the ultimate destiny of their offspring, for piglets, we learned, are born not to be loved but to be eaten.

This is the most embarrassing fact. When we bought the gilts, two pigs in pokes, we studiously avoided the connections the breeder was making between their potential for growth and the consumption of pig flesh. Other pig farmers might imagine the pork roasts and ham that rewarded their labors, but not us.

We were only thinking of ways to liberate our darlings. We knew we could do better for them than the professionals who had designed Hogs and Logs, a state of the art pig farm—prison farm, we thought— equipped with automated feed chutes, piped-in music, clever indoor plumbing, and rigid segregation.

The boars were locked up in holding pens at the far end of the lot, an enclosed structure of preformed concrete the size of two football fields. Easier on them, that way, the owner explained. That way they don't smell the sows.

Breathing in the rank smell of pig feed and manure, musk and desire, we walked nervously past cement cells twelve feet by eight feet. The doomed gilts and barrows, six to a pen, separated by their sex, faced each other mournfully. Denied their basic right to root and mate, they seemed listless, bored and hostile. The mothers and their litters were housed in farrowing cells equipped with showers. "Sows need a lotta water," their owner warned us, "one helluva lotta water. Mind that, Bob, don't let 'em dry up."

We assured him that we were building a magnificent mud hole that would quench our pigs' thirst while satisfying their natural desires. They would be able to root as well as bathe in a pool of their own construction. The pig baron just laughed.

He laughed because he knew that pigs were born to be eaten, not to be loved. He laughed because he knew that it costs too much money to keep them for any other reason. We circumvented his awful truth in the first litter when most of Sissy's children died before they became a threat to our fragile physical economy. Jessie's children, so much hardier, should have forced upon us their irreducible need for nourishment, but we were lulled into a false security over their fate by a miracle that happened this way.

Jessie's piglets were eight weeks old, scampering and prancing and somersaulting around the pig yard. Theoretically we were going to sell them to country folks who were just lining up out there to buy suckling pigs. Theoretically these country folks religiously purchased baby pigs every spring to fatten them up for the fall. I knew about this from E.B. White, whom I realized later was a city person writing about country ways at a time when the price of pork exceeded the price of pig feed.

What we learned later, through our own painful marketing research, was that country folks thought only a fool would spend the time and money to fatten up porkers when pork chops were going dirt cheap down at the local A&P. City folks would spend much more for organic free range pork, but our pigs lived in the country, where we could not give our pigs away, not even to local orphanages, unless we threw in three months of pig feed to sweeten the deal.

But at the moment, happily pig ignorant, we were merely imagining the guilt we would feel when our piglets would end up as ham to grace the table of some friendly country family down the road on Christmas day. (We would never, we had decided, sell our feeder pigs to assholes.)

And just then, just at that very moment of contemplation, somebody came to the door. A pale, somewhat flabby messenger from God drove up in a shiny silver Lincoln Continental. He wore plaid shorts, a Pocono Mountains t-shirt, and chewed energetically on a cigar. He was staying down at Buck Falls, he said, where he stayed every year, and he wanted to buy a pig. He heard at the Sunoco station that we had some.

He spoke oddly, a New Yorker mixing his street and country smarts indiscriminately. His friend down the road, a real native who actually lived in Canadensis all year long, was turning forty-five that weekend, and he thought, being an honorary good old boy, that the perfect present would be a real cute pig.

He only asked three things: he'd get the pick of the litter, we'd get the pig cleaned up, and we'd keep the entire transaction a secret. The last condition puzzled us, inspiring Molly to imagine complicated plots of animal abuse or scientific experimentation, but I now think that this buyer was merely worried that his birthday surprise would be spoiled by premature revelations. We agreed to all three demands, set a price of $25 and accompanied him to the pig shed where he chose the runt.

He returned three days later, wearing Kelly green golf slacks and a pink Izod shirt, accompanied by his wife and another couple—all equally iridescent—who wanted to see a real live pig farm. He lifted a Bloomingdale's shopping bag out of the back seat filled with one bottle of Vidal Sassoon shampoo, one boar's bristle hair brush, one Dior

Turkish towel, and a large red bow. While the Buck Hills brigade inspected the pig yard, Bob soaped up the pig, dried him off with the Dior towel, scratched his backside with the boar bristles, and tied the bow around the damp, pink neck of our first sacrifice. We had to give back the towel.

Three days later the man returned, familiar by now in his original plaid shorts, more sunburned than before. He was so tickled with the first pig that he just had to buy another. His friend was building a pigpen and, what the heck, the more the merrier. What are friends for?

"You got quite an operation here," he said, poking into the air with his cigar, "quite a little operation. You know you could make a fortune hawking these suckers in New York City." He could recognize that a big market was growing for specialty items like our pigs. "Think of all the anniversaries and birthdays," he said, "think of reformed bar mitzvahs."

This time he did not provide a towel. We shampooed up pig number two, tied on another red ribbon, and waved goodbye to the Continental, agreeing with some degree of complacency that we had indeed quite a little operation.

We never sold another pig.

It took a while for all of this to sink in. We imagined ourselves as the founders of a revolutionary movement. We would bombard the bored and guilty rich with brochures filled with engaging shots of Wilbur dancing, Jessie skating, and Sissy smiling. These irresistible images would inspire wealthy donors to adopt our pigs by mail. We could supply each New York neighborhood with its own individual pig, sending back pictures of their adopted animals running free. Free to root between the hedges that separated us all from our essential selves. If people could only learn the sweetness and the willingness to oblige that each pig possessed, if people could only understand the personal bonding possible between pigs and humans, our pigs would fly.

Around this time I found, remaindered, a paperback meditation on "hogritude" full of pig lore, mythological and biological. William

Hedgepeth's *Hog Book* stressed the physiological similarities between the flesh of the short and long pig (we're the long). Black and white photographs and delicate line drawings partial to the Hampshire celebrated pigs rooting, pigs nuzzling, pigs sleeping, pigs thinking, pigs flying, pigs marching, pigs glowing, all united in a holy struggle for self-realization.

Final snapshots revealed the fate of pigs cut off from their destiny, pigs electrocuted, stabbed, frozen, butchered. We were not alone. Pig lovers were out there.

My blindness was dazzling. If I had been a vegetarian, I might have enjoyed more credibility. But my commitment to the pigs was purely personal, one that depended upon a reciprocal relationship established between them and me on weekends and during the summer.

Meanwhile, dreaming of animal rights, I was also busy trying out Jane Grigson's recipes for pig's trotters, pig's tails, pig's brains, pig's livers, pig's kidneys, pig's hearts, pig's ears, pig's tongues, and my favorite, pig's head. (See her classic treatment of "Extremities" in *Charcuterie and French Pork Cookery*.)

I had made brawn before, when we lived in London, where eyeless pig's heads grinned down from the butcher stalls. In the Poconos they were more elusive. Country folk are funny that way. It takes city types hungry for stimulation to search out sour grass and offal. The shoppers at Dutch's Market in Newfoundland in 1983 liked their cold cuts cellophane wrapped, their bread snow white and rubbery, and their milk homogenized and government inspected. Weird folks too educated to mind about tuberculosis lapped up milk raw from the farmers—the sort of sickly looking folks, according to Bob, that floated around the White Clouds vegetarian restaurant up the road. City folks who couldn't tell the difference between a bull and a heifer if their life depended upon it.

A typical recipe from the fireman's auxiliary cook book called for one cup of mayonnaise, one pound of Velveeta cheese, one can of Campbell's mushroom soup, a half can of green beans, and a handful of Kellogg's Corn Flakes to sprinkle on the top. The local creative cooks, Frieda, who kept bees and made her own cheese, and Doc's wife, Vita, who experimented with bear hearts, elephant ears and nettles, were originally from cities. They had carried with them urban household gods and a dedication to nature methodized that puzzled their neighbors.

Perversely, I wanted to be able to buy a pig's head from the local market in order to strike a blow against white bread and Velveeta and to raise the culinary consciousness of the county. That's what I thought then, but maybe I just wanted to show off. When friends asked me why I didn't cook one of my own pig's heads, I muttered something dire about cannibalism. I badgered the butcher at Dutch's Market into procuring one for me from the slaughterhouse and arrived impatiently on a busy Saturday morning to collect it.

It gazed up at me from a plastic tray, gray and frozen. They had not removed the eyes. "I wanted it split," I explained. "I don't have a pan large enough to hold a whole head." The butcher glared at me, but sent it back to the workroom behind the counter. I could hear the sound of an electrical saw that kept stalling.

What's going on, people lined up to buy bologna wanted to know, what's taking so long? "It's her," I heard. "She wants a pig's head, and she wants it split." The crowd murmured its disapproval.

It's a good thing, I thought, that I didn't say anything about removing the eyes, although back home, hacking away at them, feeling them roll away from my probing fingers, I regretted my shyness. "What's wrong with head cheese," one woman wanted to know, "it's $2.59 a pound this week, not good enough for you?"

Finally the butcher returned, bearing two plastic trays. Two separate eyes staring out of two separate pig profiles moved the crowd to anger. "Jesus Christ, will you look at that, it's disgusting."

I clung to the halves of my head, and ran to the cash register where shoppers stopped foraging for Wonder bread and marshmallow fluff and Fritos and Miracle Whip to gather around me in sullen curiosity. I was lucky they didn't know that not five miles from my dearly purchased pig's head twenty-seven pigs were rooting away at the foundations, leaping over hot wires, and filling the sweet summer air with the essence of piggy lust, ready every one to increase and multiply.

I pretended that I didn't mind, that consistency was the hobgoblin of…some sort of mind, not mine. I had my pig head to make my brawn.

It takes two days to make brawn, and in the simmering stage smells better than anything I know, better than chutney, better than lamb daube made with a pig's foot. For hours the house fills up with the sweetness of pork, the sharpness of lemon, the earthiness of turnip and leek, and the pungent bite of cumin and garlic and mace.

Here is the recipe I used, from *The Cookery Year*, with some variations from me and from Jane Grigson.

A recipe for Brawn

One half pig's head,
8 oz. rock or sea salt
2 onions
4 shallots
2 carrots
2 turnips
12 whole allspice
Bouquet garni
4 cloves
2 blades mace
6 peppercorns
Juice of a lemon
Oil
Salt and black pepper

Variations:
  Grigson adds two leeks.

I add:
  One head of garlic, peeled
  One teaspoon of ground cumin
  One teaspoon of ground coriander

Ask the butcher to cut the pig's head in two and to remove the eyes. Scrub the portions under cold running water until thoroughly clean. Leave them to soak for 12 hours in a bowl of cold water to which 8 oz. of salt has been added.

Remove the pig's head, rinse it thoroughly in fresh water and place it in a large saucepan. Cover with fresh cold water. Bring to the boil, and cook the pig's head at near-boiling point for 2 hours or until the flesh leaves the bones easily. Remove the meat from the pan. Strip all the flesh, including the ear, tongue and brain, from the bones—it should yield approximately 2 lb. of meat. Return the bones to the pan with the cooking liquid and bring back to the boil. Meanwhile, peel and roughly slice the onions, shallots, carrots, and turnips. Add the vegetables to the boiling liquid, together with the allspice, bouquet garni, cloves, mace, peppercorns and lemon juice, garlic, cumin and coriander.

Continue boiling this stock, uncovered, for about 1 hour until the liquid has reduced to just over 1/2 pint. Remove from the heat, strain and set the liquid aside until cold. Skin the tongue and dice that and all the meat finely. Put the meat in a large bowl and work it through the fingers until thoroughly mixed, discarding any pieces of gristle.

Remove the solidified fat from the surface of the cold stock, and strain the liquid through two thicknesses of muslin (cheese cloth) into a clean pan. Season with salt and freshly ground pepper and bring to the boil. Remove the pan from the heat and stir in the chopped meat.

Brush a 2-pint tin mold with oil and spoon the brawn carefully into the mold. Firm the top of the brawn and set it aside for 1 hour. Cover the brawn with a wooden board, with a heavy weight on top, like a brick, and chill in the refrigerator for at least 24 hours.

To serve, turn the brawn out of the mold.

While the brawn chilled, I read more recipes. *Pieds de porc a la Ste-Menehould* are cooked for 48 hours until "they can be eaten bones and all. This gives three textures—crisp, gelatinous and the hard-soft biscuit of the edible bones." Ears sounded particularly inviting. "The cartilage has an agreeably contrasting bite, which goes well with the blandness of the meat."

You can see how confusing it all became. One minute I was stroking the tender, scaly point between ear and neck that pigs so love to have scratched, and the next minute I was imagining myself crunching *oreilles de porc* between my sharp shiny teeth. Nature, at least my nature, was not very easily satisfied.

By now, we were all dissatisfied. We didn't know how to complain about the big things. One December weekend, we spent twelve hours off and on trying to get an enormous Christmas tree up onto its wobbly stand. The biggest Scotch pine in the lot, ten feet tall, it thwarted our feeble attempts to erect it. Even Denny, six feet eight inches tall, couldn't do it. But we didn't know how to stop trying.

When we weren't struggling with Christmas trees, Denny and I were drinking too hard and fighting bitterly through day and night. Patrick and Molly stared at us, shellshocked, finally turning up the record player to drown out our words.

YMCA dah dah dah dah dah dah YMCA.

After that weekend, on the way back to Brooklyn, I stopped at an emergency ward for an EKG for my chest pains. The doctor told me that I wasn't having a heart attack, but had just strained my arm and chest muscles trying to keep the trunk of the tree straight. After teasing out the details of the weekend, he gave me his card and suggested that I seek counseling at a family mental health clinic.

I still have the card, buried in the inner depths of my study. I never did visit that doctor, and none of us ever complained about that weekend. Instead we rewrote it, turning it into a funny story we told on ourselves. The kids, we told ourselves, didn't complain about our fighting. But then, how could they? Instead, they said they missed being in Brooklyn. They said they were getting too old to play farmer. Patrick missed his Dungeon and Dragon battles back home; Molly missed Meredith.

They didn't say, although they knew, that somehow Flatbush, with all of its street crime, seemed a safer place to be. We had neighbors in Flatbush, neighbors who could see and hear and respond to the sounds and sights of a marriage breaking apart. Neighbors who cared about them, who might stop things before they went too far. But out here in the country no holds were ever barred. Denny and I had become scary.

But we didn't pay attention to the tremors shaking the foundation. We complained instead about the pigs, those objects not just of our desire, but also of our dissatisfaction.

Bob complained that he did not own a proper truck, the right piece of machinery to take him all over the Pocono Mountains in search of supplies for our farm. That's what he needed to solve the pig problem—the right sort of truck. He was partly right, but at the time, having watched him dump two or three worn-away vehicles onto our back lot already, we worried about investing in more equipment.

Denny and I complained about spending more money on pig feed and lumber and cortisone injections for Sissy's arthritis. And the kids complained about the pigs themselves.

Sissy's children had turned into thugs, nasty, brutish, short-tempered, lounging around the hot wire ready to lunge at anybody foolish enough to try to feed them apples. Even Wilbur—so gentle that first summer—even Wilbur was turning mean. He had taken to nipping the barrows. We built him a separate yard where he snorted his displeasure. The summer before he had soared three feet high in the air through the garage window. He landed with a triumphant snort and joined a barbecue we were having in the back yard. His strength delighted us then, and we bragged about his exploit for months—our pigs could fly. But now, remembering his leap, we boarded up the garage window and listened fearfully as he pounded his hoofs against the shed.

Only Jessie remained constant, steadily indifferent to our desires. Our initial gestures of solicitude seemed no more relevant to her than our last, fearful omissions. For she had always known that we were not pigs. Our clumsy attempts to communicate were merely tedious and dishonest encroachments.

Humans, she seemed to know, would always turn out the same in the end.

THE PIG WHO DIED

AFTER HER SECOND LITTER HAD BEEN WEANED and it started getting cold at nights, Sissy began to hobble around the pig yard. Doc asked us what we wanted to do. She has arthritis, he said, and it's incurable. We could give her cortisone for the pain, but as long as she lived in the drafty, damp shed, she'd get worse, no matter what.

"And I don't expect you to install central heating at this stage of the game." He laughed. We could slaughter her, but we couldn't get much for her meat. At her weight, she'd only be good for sausage.

"Or," he said slowly, "we could just put her out of her misery." Sissy looked up at us with her usual trust.

Sissy suffered. I am not anthropomorphizing now. When she lost the use of her right back leg, she dragged her body stiffly, as if it might break. The taut Poland China Spots sagged, crumpled reminders of her former glory. Feeding her became difficult. If we left her with the younger pigs, they would rush her, nipping and pushing her into the mud to get at her feed. She would cry out to her children, but they did not know her. Occasionally Jessie would charge the invaders, and, once or twice, she bit one of her own gilts in the leg. Most days, she remained aloof, tending her own supply of grain.

We solved the problem by quarantining Sissy with Wilbur. At first we worried about him mounting her, but we underestimated his sense of the fitness of things. After we pushed Sissy, as gently as possible, over the detached hot wire into Wilbur's yard, he trotted over to her with enthusiasm. First he sniffed her delicately with his quivering snout. But then he snorted and backed off, as if he smelled her sickness.

The entire time that Sissy stayed in his pen, Wilbur kept to himself. He wouldn't even go after her food. The two spent most of their time lying sullenly at opposite ends of the yard, their huge heads cradled in their front trotters.

All through September and most of October we kept giving Sissy the cortisone shots. It might have been more humane to kill her at once, but we couldn't make ourselves do it. Instead, we made feeble jokes about veterinary science, fantasizing over artificial hip sockets that would restore the old Sissy to us.

I think that the real reason we kept Sissy alive is that her sweetness kept the dream of the pig project alive. Without her, we would be left with a boar turning sour, an even meaner sow, and a herd of indistinguishable, dissatisfied pigs bent on rape and pillage. We would be left, finally, with ourselves—and by then "we" had become a complicated word. Denny and I were nipping and thrashing each other worse than Jessie and Wilbur put together.

Finally, in late October, we called Doc. He was not surprised, and agreed to drive over in his truck. He'd have to take her away to be disposed of, he said—as if she were spoiled meat. But then Doc had no time for sentimental euphemisms. He seemed to evaluate animals on the basis of their strength and fortitude, and, above all, their ability to endure pain. He never cared how likable they were, or how much we needed them.

On the way out of Newfoundland, he kept his own cows and pigs and ducks and chickens and horses and goats and dogs and cats higgledy-piggledy. Some animals roamed freely, nesting or rooting or sprawling all over the hills back of his house, some were cooped up, others tethered—each according to its needs.

I remember him leaning against his office door as he pulled a porcupine quill out from his own stomach. It had lodged there in a struggle with one of his dogs.

"Takes a while for them to work their way out," he said. "I'm in no hurry."

We were there with our own dog, Dixie. She too was covered in quills, another dog stupid enough to chase after a baby porcupine that had nested in one of our apple trees. We had named the porcupine Fudge.

"Fudge," Doc barked, "Fudge. You might as well go and christen every gnat and fly on the landscape while you're at it. Folks like you give nature a bad name."

This day in October, Doc gave Sissy's death his full attention. He had told us over the phone that he would just give her a little shot; it wouldn't hurt her a bit. When he arrived, however, he looked embarrassed to see Molly and her friend Meredith standing impatiently in the driveway. Patrick had stayed away that weekend; Sissy was his pig, and he couldn't stand to see her go. Doc smiled down at the girls and pulled me to one side. "Look, I'm using a gun," he said, "it's faster than any medication, and she really won't suffer. Keep them away, or," he softened, "at least make it clear to them what we're up to."

Molly knew all about guns. Denny and I had argued over them for years, but all the while we discussed their relative virtues he just kept on collecting them. I had given up by then, and tried to pretend that I didn't hear them going off. He made targets out of almost anything, once demolishing a turkey lookout in the woods with three hundred rounds of forty-five caliber ammo.

One rainy afternoon he stalked and killed a rat almost the size of a fox. First he picked it off with his rifle, blowing away half of its spine. Then he shot the rat six times with his .357 Magnum, turning it into a bloody pulp. He and Molly and Patrick buried the pieces behind the pigpen. So Molly worried, imagining that Sissy would be blown into little mangled bits.

Molly and Meredith decided that they still wanted to help bury Sissy. We followed Doc to the pig yard to collect her, sweet Sissy lying in the sun, soaking up the last strong rays of the season. The arthritis had just about paralyzed her backside, but Bob managed to get her standing by stroking her softly under her haunches. That's as far as he got because Sissy was particularly wary of the hot wire. Jessie used to charge it periodically to see if it was still worth avoiding. Not Sissy. Once she felt its force, she stayed as far away from it as she could. On or off, to Sissy it meant stunning pain and disorientation.

Bob tried to lure her over with a big bucket of feed, but she refused to budge. Even when he offered her apples, donuts and her favorite marshmallow cookies, she sat squat down on her haunches and glared. We all took turns wheedling and coaxing, until Doc went back to his truck and brought out a rope. He made a slipknot and, in three quick movements, forced Sissy's mouth open, jammed the rope between her jaws, and brought it around her snout. Then he pulled it tight and began dragging her out of the pen.

Even in her emaciated state, Sissy outweighed Doc by a couple of hundred pounds. But he dug into the mud and pulled her after him. He grunted and she squealed and he swore and she cried and he won. Soon she was sprawled against the pick up truck, shaking and wheezing. The younger pigs shoved and pushed each other, smelling her fear and imitating her forlorn and outraged noises. Wilbur and Jessie stared at us sullenly from their separate pens. We all looked at our feet, even Doc, who was working at getting his breath back.

We had to force Sissy up a ramp onto the truck. By now she had turned obstinate out of pain as well as fear. Her struggle against Doc had forced her to use the arthritic parts she had been favoring. Since she wouldn't move on her own, we pushed her from behind, while Doc pulled her straining snout forward. I could feel her warm, shrunken haunches quivering and heaving beneath me. It took us about forty minutes to get her up and into the truck bed. Even as she flailed and groaned and rolled her eyes, she never lunged at any of us and, one terrible moment, when we all rested between pushes, she licked Bob's hand, making him cry.

After Doc secured Sissy, he jumped into his pickup truck, promising that it would be easier now. "This was the hard part," he said, but we didn't believe him.

Denny, the girls and I followed in our car, but Bob stayed behind. He wiped his tears away with his hard, horny hand. "I can't do it," he said, "I'm sorry, but I just can't."

It was about four in the afternoon. Already the sky was turning lavender and orange. Ducks were flying south overhead and the country unfolded before us, plowed up and turned over, officially put to rest for the winter. We could hear geese honking. The corn had been cut down, now, and most of the haystacks had been brought in. The last frost had withered all but the hardiest weeds. Nature was shrinking down into its cold essential self.

I thought then about Demeter. The Hog Book said that the pig had been her sacred animal, commemorated in a three-day festival called Thesmophoria. Live pigs were shut up into sacred caverns where they starved to death. They were exhumed a year later, their decayed flesh becoming fertilizer, promising bumper crops.

As we set forth to bury Sissy in a cornfield, I was angry at my glib talent for making the appropriate symbolic connection. I wanted to attend to Sissy, the individual pig, but she was already becoming a seasonal casualty, a footnote to the Golden Bough. I could never tell these things to the kids. They hated it when I turned the real into the academic.

Worse still, my desire to personalize this individual pig in the first place, to translate her out of her Hogs and Logs destiny, had created her too personal, pathetic state of arthritic dependency. For Sissy, I knew, had somehow believed the promises that we had sung into her tender spotted ear that first summer in the pig yard. We would all live together, safe and free, and we would never, never die.

We bounced over the ruts and gullies of Stony Lonesome Road and wound around nameless dirt lanes to pull into the cornfield. Decay was hanging heavy in the air. The sweet stench of rotting corn was overpowered by the sharper smell of goldenrod festering at the edge of the field.

We approached Doc's truck warily, waiting for instructions.

Sissy was moaning in the back and thrashing her legs stiffly against the side. But even in that state of extremity, she stopped her crying when she saw us and grunted softly. Doc pulled out two shovels from the cab and handed one to Denny. He walked fast, into the middle of the field.

"This is where it gets tricky," he said. "You got to bury deep down, and you don't want to be too close to the edge. Bears come out of the woods and dig 'em up at night."

He started right in, lunging forward, thrusting down, and wrenching up to fling the soft clods of dirt behind him. He made Denny look clumsy struggling with his shovel. After about ten minutes, I pestered him into giving me a turn. I was worse, stabbing at earth hard and heavy on my hands. While we spelled each other, Doc kept on bringing up dirt, bending down with rhythmic grace to pile it high behind him.

As we dug the hole, the girls picked blasted goldenrod and burdock, spiky white daisies and rusty weeds that had no name. We were all silent then, except for Doc, who kept talking about the bears, and Sissy. She kept looking at us hard while she made short snuffling sounds, as if she were sobbing. And finally it was time. The grave, about four feet deep and six feet long, waited for us to do something.

We followed Doc to the truck. He reached into his glove compartment and pulled out a cardboard box. We all held our breath as he carefully removed a shiny black Colt .45 from its stiff, rustling tissue paper. Denny and Doc traded compliments about their mutual knowledge of guns in that terse, irritating way men have, while Doc took two bullets out of his shirt pocket, pulled out the clip, and loaded the gun.

"Now Molly," he said, "I just want to tell you, it's the best way. The medicine takes longer, a good twenty minutes, and all that while poor Sissy'd be flailing around and kicking her bad leg and hurting herself. This way's fast. Do you understand?"

Molly shook her head yes. Molly, pale beneath her freckles, clutched Meredith's hand. I tried to hold onto her, but she shook me off. The girls stood together, goldenrods and daisies braided into their hair, eleven year old priestesses presiding over an ancient rite.

Doc gave Denny the gun to hold and went around to the back.

It was easy to get Sissy to roll out of the truck. On the ground, she shook her head vigorously, happy to be back with her friends in this alien field. Ready to root, hampered only slightly by the slipknot, she walked slowly over the ploughed up field full of succulent corn stalks and fat, sluggish corn borers. For the moment, she was truly in pig heaven.

"No hot wire," Molly whispered, bending to pat her on the side.

We finally reached the hole. Sissy sniffed around it. For a terrible moment, I thought that she would fall into her own grave, but she hesitated, cautious as ever, and looked up at us. Doc took the gun from Denny and inspected it idly to give us time to hug her. Finally, giving the gun and the pig one last look, Doc asked us, politely, to step back. Too quickly he grabbed Sissy under the throat, pulled back her head, held the gun against her ear and shot her dead. She crumpled down into a heap, and slowly, inexorably, always obliging, rolled to the edge of her grave and slid down its side to land on her back with a soft thud.

Molly broke the silence with a question. "Can I throw in the flowers now?"

"Hold on a minute, Doc cried. He ran back to his truck and returned swinging a black, stiff hairy object.

"Dead cat," he grinned, "I lost her last week. Hell, don't worry. Sissy won't mind. That old cat'll keep her company."

And mumbling something about bears, Doc lowered himself into the grave. We watched him place the cat gently under Sissy's front trotter. She looked ridiculously maternal, solicitous to the end, nursing one last ungrateful child. And we laughed uneasily while Molly and Meredith covered the pig and the cat with their flowers and weeds.

It was quiet as we filled up the hole, stopping every once in a while to look out onto the field. The sky was dark purple now, and just beyond the goldenrods the bears were beginning to gather invisibly in the gloom. Doc offered Molly and Meredith a ride back in his truck. Molly grinned in triumph, "wait till Patrick hears about this," she said, nudging Meredith. Both girls began to giggle and gloat, but suddenly they stopped themselves. They looked as if they were going to cry, Molly in earnest, Meredith in sympathy.

"Wait," Doc called, hurrying into his cab for one last treasure. Two smooth metal bars clanked. He drew them together and offered them to the girls. "I bet you can't pull those beauties apart. See, they're magnets. Strong enough to pull the barbed wire right out of a cow's stomach. Now cows, cows are really stupid, not like pigs. Not one bit. Catch Sissy choking on barbed wire." He left the girls in the back of the truck playing with the magnets, and he drove off with them down the road.

We followed after down Stony Lonesome Road, and we watched for Sissy, golden in the dying sun, riding high in her low sweet chariot. We looked out for bears, but only saw one dead possum at the side of the highway and a fat suspicious looking raccoon scuttling across our headlights.

Pigs are not shed so easily. While we dreamed of Sissy ascending into heaven, back at the house too many live pigs (including Jessie's new litter) were waiting to be fed. Snorting and shoving and rooting and wailing, they would be undermining the precarious foundation of their pig shed and uprooting the raspberry bushes growing next to the yard. If only they would charge the hot wire, head for the highway, and be picked up by innocent motorists looking for outsized pets. Or maybe they could be stolen in the night by Satanists, or hijacked in the early morning by vagrant meat packers. Better still, they could escape into the Pocono Mountains where they would roam free and live on hips and haws. That's what they eat in pastorals—hips and haws and an occasional acorn.

But our pigs, having developed a taste for Bob's over-ripe nectarines and yogurt past sell-by-date, were not so naive. Whenever they broke through the hot wire, charging wantonly into the apple trees, scattering chickens and dogs, cats and ducks before them, they merely played with the idea of escape. What they really wanted to do was to trample, uproot, shit and piss their way up to the edge of the road. They would stop there to confer a while before trotting back to their yard for a proper, civilized dinner of bananas and sterilized grains.

One pig, the most pathetic victim of our kindness, never rampaged. I speak now of Snowflake, an orphan that Bob picked up somewhere in his travels between Newfoundland and Stroudsburg. After two years, he had worn out three trucks in search of stale food thrown out behind the local grocery stores. He would bring back cartons of soggy corn flakes, bushel baskets of spoiled tomatoes, and cases of sour cream. On one of his food runs, he brought back a suckling pig. She was a Yorkshire, like Wilbur, pure white with pink eyes, shy and demure. Her eager pleasing ways reminded us all of Sissy in the early days. How could we say no?

Bob built her a large wooden box six feet by six feet, four feet high. "A holding tank," he called it. Snowflake's temporary home until she could take care of herself. She was just a little pig, you see, with no mother to protect her from Jessie's and Sissy's ruffians. Why, she wouldn't last ten minutes in the pig yard, he warned. And so, immured in the garage, unable to root, unable to walk, she became a big, helpless toy—one who could perform two functions, standing still or lying down. Well, three if you added in her best trick. She could jump up eagerly to greet us, her front trotters scraping the top of her box. Snowflake could stay in this position, precariously balanced, for approximately two wobbly minutes. Two minutes filling us with guilt. What were we doing, we asked Bob, asked ourselves, to this poor creature?

As we feared, the temporary box became her permanent home. Without exercise, she grew immensely fat and flabby, a sequestered virgin protected not just from the younger pigs' violence, but also from Wilbur's lust. Whenever I watched our prisoner swelling with inactivity, I remembered with shame our heady schemes of liberation formed that day so long ago at Hogs and Logs.

Bob and I fought over Snowflake, long and hard that last winter. After Wilbur turned mean, Bob spent more time talking to the penned-up gilt. "She sure does know her name," he'd say, projecting onto her an intelligence that could never be tested. "Do you get a load of the way she jumps up when she hears my car come up the drive?"

Snowflake would indeed be waiting for Bob, her bloated face upturned, bobbing between her clean, useless trotters. I suppose that you could call her ability to balance herself on her hind legs, front trotters pressed against the rim of the box, a talent. Bob certainly did. He also adored her compliance, pretending that it flowed freely from her. But her cloistered innocence depressed me. The kids wouldn't go near her.

45

I wanted her gone, I kept saying, I wanted them all gone, all but Wilbur and Jessie, they could stay, but the rest were out the door. Bob began setting up meetings with various folk burdened with dreams and limitations of their own. "I got this guy up Promised Land way," Bob would whisper, eyes gleaming, "and he's dying to take five, maybe even six, but his truck keeps breaking down, and his wife isn't all that certain. Now if we had a truck, well then, we'd be home clear."

Then there was the rich guy near Sky Top, "he stopped by the other day and just fell in love with Snowflake, but I said no sale there, she's our sweetheart, but he'd be willing to take one or two others off our hands, but then his son went and got killed in a motorcycle accident, if that isn't the luck."

Luck ran from bad to worse. Families in the mood for pork would mysteriously move to Wyoming (PA that is), or would get not so mysteriously divorced. One potential buyer fell off a roof and broke a leg, while another farmer down by Canadensis was all ready to pick up three of Jessie's finest when his house burned to the ground. I started to feel responsible.

Responsibility was difficult to locate. However hard we worked to sell the pigs, we worked even harder to protect ourselves from their ultimate end. Bob's failures to sell the pigs satisfied, for a while, this ambivalence. Each time a future farmer fell off his roof, we were and were not doing something about *it*—the final solution to what we called *the pig problem*.

We started to feel comfortable dwelling in the polite shallows of euphemistic, opaque language. We were not planning to kill our pigs, ignoble offspring of Sissy and Jessie and Wilbur. We were only going to dispose of them. *The Foxfire Book* offered cunning country ways to stick pigs, but we were unwilling to get so close to the blood draining out of limp pig carcasses.

Snowflake, quivering, abject, reproaching me with her lonely, cramped and vacant state, goaded me into action. I started to avoid country weekends, knowing that at the end of the journey, as we pulled into the drive, we would hear her heavy body straining and thrusting against her prison.

"Come on over and see Snowflake," Bob would say. "She's waiting for you."

Her patient endurance made me ashamed of myself. I was determined to free her—but how? It became almost impossible to imagine a "free" Snowflake rooting happily in the pig yard. The yard itself would need to be "free" of the "problem" that kept her imprisoned—the problem of all of those other nameless boisterous pigs. If only we could get rid of the young ones, the brutes, each one weighing in at about two to three hundred pounds. Then we could release Snowflake from her box. She could live with Jessie, not happily, perhaps, who could be happy with such a mean sow nipping and tugging? But she would have a better life, with room for once to breathe and root.

We began to plan a stripped down farmyard consisting of Wilbur in one pen, Jessie and Snowflake in the other: our peaceable kingdom. We didn't say that we would sacrifice the bigger pigs to save one little one. We said that we would be solving the pig problem. I was starting to feel like a Nazi, a nice one, the kind of Nazi who played Schubert on her violin.

I took over the marketing myself, reminding everybody grimly that we could expect no more angelic adopters of piglets, no orphanages looking for pet barrows. With Doc's help, I made a list of meat packers in Pennsylvania. Then I obtained a swineherd number from the State of Pennsylvania. Number S79 and began making my business calls. "Sooooooeeeee," one packer sang out high and clear on his answering machine. "Nobody's here right now, but just leave your oink at the end of the beep, snort, snort."

In spite of their initial oinks, the meat packers were uniformly kind and gentle. None of them laughed at me outright. Most times, they clucked sympathetically at my pig problem and commiserated over the rising cost of grain. But I learned, over and over, that our pigs were not young enough, not small enough, and not numerous enough.

"Now if we only had two hundred," I'd hear, "why then I'd be there tomorrow with my trucks, but I can't pick up little bitty orders like yours. I'm not running a charity, you know. You don't want me to go broke. Not worth the drive over and back, not even if they were free. And besides, they'd be way too tough. You want a small pig, a tender pig, not some tough old rhino of a pig that's got to be ground up into sausage. Where's the profit in that?"

Profit never did reveal its mysteries. Jessie's newest piglets received even less respect. Too tender, too small, too risky. Meat packers wanted their pigs tender and solid. If I managed to fatten up the babies and got back to them in a couple of months, maybe, just maybe, they'd be interested. I started to dream now of battalions of pigs executing a fancy goose step, pigs parading in sharp, snappy lines across our five acres, pigs holding bayonets before them as they ran us off the land into the woods.

One day in December, I left one more message on one more meat packer's machine. A woman returned my call within the hour. Her husband was picking up some pigs near Scranton, she said, but she could speak for him. When I told her my story, she didn't cluck sympathetically and, when I finished, she was silent for a while. "Twenty bucks a head," she said. "And you help load them on the truck."

Bob had been asking seventy, and expecting fifty. "Twenty-five," I countered. "They're real good pigs." She waited, cleared her throat, and offered twenty-three fifty. "We'll be by for them next weekend," she promised.

Bob was furious. He would lose face up at the Sunoco station if he let his friends know that his pigs could only bring down twenty-five a head. His pigs, the finest in the northeast, not garbage pigs, not by a long shot, his pigs deserved better. And his brother-in-law, what on earth would he think? Worse still, what would he say?

"Lie," I told him, "tell them we got eighty bucks a head."

"Lie, Carol? Lie? What kind of people do you think we are up here anyway? This isn't New York City."

But I wouldn't listen. I reminded him that he had already added a lying $1.50 to our price for his own purposes. And I arranged for the pigs to be picked up the next weekend.

Bob turned crafty all of a sudden. "If we're really gonna do this," he said, "let's at least get some pork chops and sausages out of this tragedy. Nothing I like better than fresh ham. If we're killing off the pigs, we might as well benefit from the hardness of our hearts." He knew a local slaughterhouse over near Wyoming famous for their smoked bacon. If we kept out Jessie's new litter and fattened them up just a few more weeks, we'd be eating pork roast by Christmas.

Home smoked slabs of bacon. Pork roast with the crackling left on. *Noisettes de Porc aux Pruneaux de Tours.* Blood pudding. I found myself harboring an irresistible desire to eat our pigs. Indeed, I argued, not to eat them would be hypocritical. Here we were, selling our children up the river while we barbecued somebody else's ribs from Dutch's Market. Some fateful day we could find ourselves eating Sissy's first child unawares, juicy Emma neatly wrapped in cellophane, $1.29 a pound. How could such ignorance be moral? It was time, I kept saying, to get real.

My posture of self-righteous cannibalism didn't support me for long, but it did get me through the next weekend of pig management. The meat packer arrived with a truck too big for our driveway. He was appalled by the primitive nature of our operation. "No ramps," he kept muttering, "not one fucking ramp. Do they expect me to carry the suckers on my back?"

But he was, most of the time, quite civil, and became towards the end of the day positively benevolent. He patronized us mercilessly for our deficiencies, but by then we knew how much we deserved his scorn.

Bob and Denny and our meat packer, with a little help from the kids and me, pushed and shoved and pulled and lugged twenty pigs onto his truck. I can still see Patrick, pale and skinny, full of mud and anxiety, hanging onto a Hampshire barrow, while Molly turned away, trying not to cry.

Each time I pressed my hand against a straining, frightened haunch, I realized that I no longer knew one pig by name. Their anonymity shamed me even as it preserved my dubious intentions. The little pigs left behind would be easier to distinguish, but since we would be eating them by New Year's Eve, naming them seemed a waste of time and spirit. We tacitly decided to ignore them as much as possible while they served out their term.

The meat packer drove off with our pigs rushing and shoving against one another. I watched them snorting and salivating into each other's ears. I could have known them, I thought, and in another place, another time, each one of them could have been as dear and as witty as Sissy or Jessie, each one could have been fully realized by me. *Being realized* by me, I wondered. Was that their purpose?

I made myself stop justifying what had just taken place. I made myself look hard instead at the driveway filled with pig shit leading to the curiously empty pig yard. It had become a wasteland of ruts and mud holes beginning to freeze. Wilbur snorted, Jessie rooted, and Snowflake breathed heavily in her box.

It was too quiet. It was over.

Jessie's last litter arrived December nineteenth in white paper wrappers. Each one cost seventy dollars to butcher. We laid only two of them down in the freezer. The other four had been divided up between Doc and Bob. I unwrapped each and every little white package, and checked over the hams and roasts and ribs, the shoulders, the smoked butts, the slabs of bacon, the pounds and pounds of sausages, some linked, some bulk. No heads—I couldn't handle them in the end. No feet, no tails, no kidneys, no livers, and no tongues. No blood.

Our butchered pigs reminded me in their sterility and impersonality of the cellophane wrapped variety we found at Dutch's, and that was just as well. It was bad enough looking at Jessie's daughter's ribs.

With nervous sentimentality, I decided to bite the bullet. I would serve pork roast for New Year's Eve to our good friends from New York. Since Tom and Nadina knew the pigs, they would understand the solemnity of the meal.

I scored the fat with cloves of garlic sliced thin, and rubbed the meat all over with thyme and cumin and olive oil. The roast lay in a rack balanced precariously over red onions and potatoes as small as I could find.

One half hour before the roast was finished, I added Macintosh apples halved, unpeeled, face down to sputter in the pork grease. The house filled with the odor of pork and apple and onion and cumin and guilt.

Dressed up for the occasion in a pale silk blouse the color of Snow-flake, I took the best dishes from the cupboard, and unwrapped the Waterford crystal that we hadn't used since our first anniversary. We would eat with candles, I announced, and we'll use the tablecloth. And would Patrick and Molly please set the table?

I carried the roast out to the table and set it on the corner, where I would sit. I was the carver in the family, such a liberated woman; I would be the one cutting into Jessie's children. What I didn't notice was the way that Patrick had set the table. He had wanted to make it, he explained later, an extra special occasion. That's why he decided to place the candlesticks on each corner of the rectangular top. I didn't notice this change until I bent over the roast to begin carving.

As my right breast brushed ever so softly against the candle, my silk blouse burst into flames. I can still remember looking down at my breast blazing; the orange and blue flames leaping up to caress me. I could not feel the fire, although I had become part of it. I could only observe it, and remember saying, most uncharacteristically, "oh my goodness." Not *fuck*, not *shit*, just *goodness*. Mine.

I watched my friends and family staring at me staring at them, I watched them and then me, mysteriously paralyzed that night. I might still be there, on fire, if Denny hadn't jumped up, reached forward, and with one push of his large, hard hand, snuffed out the flames. I stood there, still unable to move, looking down at the huge hole in my pale silk blouse the color of Snowflake. And at my breast, barely covered by my singed, flesh colored brassiere. I stared at my friends and family open mouthed, wide eyed, and excused myself the best I could to change into a tee shirt and resume carving.

We ate every bite of that roast that New Year's Eve night, but we never touched another white package of pig. And for all I know, they are still buried deep in the freezer, burning bright in their crystals of ice, waiting underground with Sissy for their resurrection.

COLLATERAL DAMAGE

EXCEPT FOR THE PIGS, and they were many, the rest of the farm animals fared pretty well. When we moved away two years later, we gave away the cats (excellent mousers), the ducks and the chickens and the goats and the rabbits to neighbors who probably gave them the best lives that they could manage. I don't worry too much about them. It's the others that I worry about—those innocent victims of our acts of random kindness.

The problem with writing about animals is the hierarchy that always intrudes upon the subject itself. When I write about animals, I declare a certain degree of superiority over the subject at hand, the animal itself. Even when I insist that each animal is dearer and shrewder and more sensitive than any human could ever be, it also becomes clear that I own these creatures. I can even eat some of them. The entire writing scheme threatens to become dishonest. In fact, it is dishonest.

What I call "the others" are the animals that I still worry about, the ones who came to bad—or at least uncertain—ends. Their stories can be confusing because they are so often intertwined. There was Dixie, the beautiful Akita, and of course Rosie, who was still partly ours, on weekends, and there was Tuxedo the cat, who lived with us in the city.

But first, I want to think about the smallest of the animals, the early ones that didn't quite fit, before we even imagined the pigs.

In the beginning there was Guinea. I was reminded of her when I traveled through Peru in 1987. Indian women sat on street corners offering up sheaves of long, slender, spiky grass. I asked our guide what they were selling. "Food," he said, "food for the guinea pigs. The Indians keep them in their homes. They scurry back and forth all over the floor, happy, playing with the children, and then one day, phffft, they find themselves in the stew."

Our Guinea ran loose and free, squeaking and shitting all over five floors of the house in London on Chapel Street. We bought her, after great debate, on Halloween night, 1976. Patrick was seven, Molly four. Denny was working in London, and would be for almost four more years. We were tagging along, all suffering from a certain sense of exile, and we were hungry for animal life. We needed something to hold on to and to stroke.

I suspected then, but decided not to know, that both kids had allergies. I worked at ignoring the all too obvious signs, the way that mold made Patrick wheeze and, more dramatically, the way that every time Molly got near a pony she broke out into terrible, weeping eczema. Nonetheless, she gamely rode a fat, old pony named Paint slowly up and down the sandy paths in Hyde Park. We colluded together, the kids and me, trying hard not to acknowledge the way her nose dripped, her eyes, bright red, filled with hot tears, the way she began to wheeze by the end of her hired hour.

I decided not to see that she had allergies, because if she did, she'd be repeating my own childhood—all those shots, all those overnights I ruined with my asthma attacks, all those bad grades in PE. I couldn't even play croquet without wheezing. And it would be my fault for giving her my genes.

So when we finally stopped the pony lessons, we bought our guinea pig. It was so small, we imagined, so easy to contain—just a harmless, hairless creature waving happily from its hygienic cage. Almost invisible.

We needn't have purchased a cage at all. Guinea spent most of her time being carried from room to room where she would be released to forage for signs of organic life—ours. For such a dim little creature, she was highly socialized. Her favorite spot was behind Denny's desk, where wedged between his paper files she nibbled contentedly at our tax records and shed her countless strands of hair. Every afternoon I would find Patrick and Molly breaking out in eczema from Guinea's fur and dander, lying close to the space heater. They'd be watching Blue Peter on the telly, while Guinea climbed all over them. We thought she thought that they were her mountains. Occasionally she grazed in their hair.

She was not a particularly interesting animal, but she was ours, the first family pet. We mythologized her fidelity. Whenever we climbed up the five flights of stairs to bed, inadvertently leaving her behind, she would squeak loudly to proclaim her existence, a regular Lassie ready to cover hundreds of miles to track us home. We decided that any squeak whatsoever was a sign of her intelligence. You had only to look into her eyes, so soft and benevolent, to realize that somewhere an understanding lurked that we were determined to cultivate. "Guinea, Guinea, come to me, be my love and you'll be free," we sang to her as the long dull winter afternoons turned into even longer, duller nights.

When we moved to New York, we needed to get a doctor's certificate to carry her into the country. That's when we learned, for five pounds, her sex and her health (excellent), and received a certificate to hand to the immigration officials. We were flying from London to Chicago to stay with my parents before going on to New York. The flight lasted, for one reason or another, fifteen hours. The food and bar service ended somewhere around the ninth hour.

For at least six hours, one or the other kid would moan, "Guinea, what can she be doing locked in the hold of the plane?" Guinea was safe, of course, "warm and cozy inside her wooden box," I would answer over and over. The box was supplied by the airline for twenty-five pounds. (Her flight cost another twenty-five pounds, without the movie.) "Guinea, guinea," they wailed, "How will you survive this night?"

Once on the ground, Guinea safe, once finally in place in Brooklyn, we decided to investigate Molly's allergies in earnest. Her red, angry reactions to the scratch tests marking her skinny little arms proclaimed all the reasons that we could not keep Guinea. Molly cried, Patrick cursed, and I tried to hide. As I had feared, it was decided that I was the guilty one. It was my gene that kept her from happiness.

A neighbor across the street, sweet, ironic, and hard working, taught sex education to some of Brooklyn's most difficult high school students. Carol, for that was her name, agreed to take Guinea on as a special pet. Molly could visit her, any time, and take her for walks, she promised. Assured that Guinea would be fed, watered and exercised, Molly gradually stopped making her visits of nostalgic inspection.

Guinea died sometime during the summer of 1982. We were in the Poconos at the time, and didn't learn about her death until Christmas, when we all got together at Lena's for eggnog. After Molly quizzed Carol on the burial service, we tacitly agreed to forget about her fate, sweet Guinea squeaking between the files.

But years later, when I was in Peru, I was struck by the indeterminacy of our Guinea's ending. I ate one night a perfectly roasted guinea pig, whole, served without the head. Earlier that day at the Cuzco Cathedral, I had seen the image of a frail familiar creature lying on its back, feet pointed straight up in the air, dominating the center of a colonial painting of "The Last Supper." Imagine that. Christ's last meal was a guinea pig: a *Conejillo de Indias*. However sacred, roasted guinea pig tasted like baby pig, sweet and tender, reminding me, as I chewed, of the others.

I will say from the start that I never ate the newts. They and the turtles were the only pets that passed the allergy test. We kept them in the basement rec room in Brooklyn from 1979 until we moved in 1984. The newts swam restlessly around our murky fish tank, primeval cannibals chewing on each other's tails and limbs. Each morning they would drag themselves onto the rock to display the carnage of the night before. Stubby arms grasped the slippery, moss-covered mound; gnawed tails waved at nothing in particular.

Their sublime impersonal energy fascinated me, so dark and evil, unconnected to any other form of life I have known. We gave them away to the movers when we moved to Brookline.

I'm afraid that I killed the turtles. Anyone might have. They were large, truculent, boring. We fed them chopped hamburger and lettuce. I remembered as I watched them devour their dinner how much I had hated the reptile house at the Brookfield Zoo in Chicago. Our turtles gave off that same fetid smell.

The pet shop owner told us to bathe them once a week in the tub. That would have been fun, I thought, imagining them swimming back and forth in grateful abandon. But they shit with abandon instead, in long, stinking turds, sometimes half a foot long. After their evacuation they would submerge themselves to lurk sullenly underwater, refusing to come up for air.

I don't think that I actually planned to kill the turtles. I thought that they needed to go into hibernation in the winter. I could remember reading that in a library book about turtles. Carefully covering them over with straw, I placed them in a box upstairs in the cold attic and left them there until the spring. In March 1980, when we drew back the straw, we found only their shells.

To make up for my criminal neglect, Patrick and Molly and I gave those turtles a most ambitious funeral. We buried them in the back yard, but first sang hymns, *Rock of Ages* and *Swing Low Sweet Chariot*; then we covered their grave with fish food and flowers. Neighborhood cats kept unearthing the shells. For months they would rattle around the lawn, grim reminders of our mortality.

That fall, a friend from England visited. He went for what he called a stroll in the garden and apparently ended up chatting to the tortoises. That's what he called them.

"So very peaceful, the tortoise," he exulted, "one of God's masterpieces. They seem to absorb one's every word. If only I could have such creatures in my garden in Islington."

"Oh, but you can, Philip," I said, and offered him the empty shells. He became very frosty.

It's impossible to stop personalizing the animals. Guinea squeaks out her devotion, and even the newts possess a lurid, heroic glamour.

I killed the animals that refused to reflect our desires, just as we eliminated and even ate Sissy's children for their anonymous, callous brutality. We loved the animals to death.

THE CAT WHO BIT MY FOOT

I CAN'T EVEN REMEMBER WHEN WE FIRST GOT THE CAT. Those years in Brookline are like that. I only remember movement. The first year, 1984, blurs into one continual shuttle between Boston and New York. I came up for tenure that year at NYU, but was living in an entirely different state, literally and figuratively.

The second year settles into uneasy stasis. I got tenure, but also got a job at Tufts, in Boston, which I took to try to mend things, to make the family work. But whatever the year, in Brookline, from 1984 to 1988, I mostly remember pain. Two years of gum surgery, Patrick's two broken hands, Molly's wallpaper covered over in graffiti, my two scratched corneas and, of course, the cat bite.

But just when did we get the cat? Nobody remembers.

I know who gave him to us. He was a Marxist cat, one of Peter's many litters. Peter's daughter Kate and Molly were close friends then. Kate was spunky and independent. Once, after the kids broke Molly's four-posted pineapple bed that we'd moved from the country by jumping up and down on its sagging frame, Kate tried to fix it with a hammer and some nails. She failed, but I liked her for the effort, and was glad to have her cat.

And I liked it being Peter's. Like me, he taught eighteenth century literature, specializing in the London hanged. We would sit together on the back deck drinking beer, talking about dead bodies, anatomies, and revolution while we watched the cat stalk birds.

Certainly there were reasons for keeping the cat. He was small and black and dapper, with white paws, a distinguished white ruff around his neck and a white spot on his forehead. He possessed a formal elegance, a haughtiness bordering on conceit that attracted me. He tended to stay aloof, keeping one wary eye on the back door. But on occasion, he would run wild with affection, purring, moaning and shuddering with delight. He would butt us then with his lowered head, and rub vigorously against our various body parts, demanding that we stroke him.

These attacks of affection were short lived. He would catch himself in the middle of an embrace, shake his head impatiently, and stride off, tail waving dangerously behind him. He could not be called back. Anyone foolish enough to follow would be scratched or bitten.

Because he looked debonair, I called him Tuxedo. Because he was unfriendly, Molly called him Welly. Because he grew mean and incontinent, Patrick called him Turd.

The cat of course did not answer to any of the above, and eventually, when he ran away, took a fourth name, Midnight, from his dazzled new owners.

The first and third names are obvious enough, but Molly's needs some explaining. The word "Welly" comes from the word welfare. To be on welfare or to be in need of welfare—indeed, to be needy at all —was to be ridiculously debased in the eyes of the neo-social-Darwinist adolescents hanging around our house in 1985. Perhaps, now that I think of it, neocon heartlessness began on our back deck, practiced by children informed by Star Wars and Dungeons and Dragons. Who knew? All I understood then was that "welly" had become a term of abuse, as in "oooh, stripes and plaids together, that's so welly."

When I finally decoded the word's meaning, I gave lectures on the politics of poverty that nobody listened to. Molly and her friends had no use for failure and even less tolerance for left wing politics. Having a social conscience was almost as bad as wearing Birkenstocks with socks.

Their resistance was complicated by their own social positions. Most of them did not fit the affluent Brookline profile, and were busy not preparing for college and perfecting the subtle nuances of a South Boston accent.

"Maaaaaaah," Molly would say, "I'm awwwwhf to baaaah some haeahhh spray. Seeyaaa lataahhh."

At first, I insisted upon calling the cat Tuxedo, not Welly, but was finally worn down by Molly's persistence and Patrick's defection. He continued to use Turd in private moments of anger, but he sided with Molly in public. Once, after the cat got into a serious fight, Molly and I took him to Brookline Animal Hospital. She registered the animal as Welly.

"What an unusual name," said the nurse. "What does it stand for?"

"Wellington," I answered, "Wellington. You know, the duke."

"Oh," she said, "like in the beef?"

I know why we got the cat. I was trying to make up for the losses. We left so many things behind in the move to Boston in 1987. Our very departure was violent and unexpected and, in retrospect, fatal.

The move sprang from Denny's ambition and my weakness. He had been restless in his job for a long while. The country house had occupied him those first few summers, but when the pig project got out of hand, it became more of a nuisance than a haven, and fed his discontent all the more. That last year in New York he would arrive home in a manic state, pour us beakers of Wild Turkey and spin tales of corporate woe.

He talked and I listened, but I didn't pay enough attention. I was up for tenure that following year, trying to finish writing a book about the body in Swift and Defoe. I would be thinking about plagues and cemeteries and wet nurses and he would be thinking about the bottom line.

Sometimes it seemed as if we were talking about the same things. I was writing about what Swift called "The Dearness of Things." He used the word "dearness" to describe economic cost, the way that life could become so "dear," so expensive, that the Irish might just be driven to fatten up their own babies to sell at the market. Cannibalism, Swift argued, pulling our reluctant legs, cannibalism could become an extreme solution to the Irish famines. All the Irish had to do was to sacrifice their dearest assets, their children.

Meanwhile, Denny was talking about his own hunger. He couldn't stand being stuck in a job taking him nowhere. He had to move forward, even if he sacrificed us in the process.

Now it seems almost inevitable, but, at the time, his decision to move us all to Boston shocked us. We responded to it dully, mechanically, as if we were living under water. No—more as if we were all frozen. Not much was known about PTSD then, but I think we all had it. We were scared and angry and we felt helpless.

Not Denny. Chaos seemed to drive him forward then, up and onward to the next exciting plateau. He received what seemed to be the perfect job offer from a mythical figure, one of the world's richest men. How could he say no? How could we not say yes please? Why wouldn't we want to hang out with the ridiculously wealthy, sail on enormous yachts and drink bottles of Montrachet, and fly through the air in helicopters? How could we reject our manifest destiny?

There was no negotiating, no staying behind for one more year in Brooklyn. That's all I needed, I argued, for this was the year I was coming up for tenure. But no, he said, we all had to move together. No exceptions.

Now, of course, it is clear that it would have been far better to break up our marriage, break it up then, break it up into little jagged pieces. But I didn't understand anything then. I was dumbfounded.

When we left Brooklyn, we also left Newfoundland behind. It was too far from Boston for weekend visits. Besides, keeping the farm going all year round to use it for only two months a year would be too expensive, far too dear.

What we left behind, besides Doc and Bob and Aggie were: three country cats grown too wild and predatory to adjust to the placid civility of Brookline, three pigs, two goats, three Peking ducks, twelve mallards, six chickens and the countless rabbits. Most important of all, we left behind Rosie. And when we gave her up, we lost part of our soul. Why couldn't we take her with us, you might ask? She wasn't as unwieldy as a pig. She would have settled into Brookline in no time at all.

But we could never forget that Rosie was on loan to us. She really belonged to Bob and Aggie. Molly never forgave us for backing down in the wake of Aggie's enormous need. But how could we ever forget Aggie's burns and her scars? Who could overlook the price she paid for feeding our dear little dog all of those innards?

So when it came time to leave the country for good, we left Rosie behind, panting and whining and wagging her tail. She had become too bloated from Aggie's lashings of gizzards and chicken liver to prance around on her hind legs anymore.

And by this time we had our own dog, ours alone, Dixie, the beautiful, stubborn Akita. But "I hate her," Molly said about Dixie, "she sucks."

And Dixie growled at Rosie. Once she nipped Rosie on the leg. Another reason to leave Rosie behind.

Before we sold the country house, we brought Rosie back with us to Brooklyn for one week to see how she would like urban living. We worried about city traffic, but that didn't faze her at all. Dixie fazed her. Snapping and growling, she scared Rosie to death when they were together in the city. This surprised us because the two dogs had always gotten along in the country. In fact, Dixie usually gave into Rosie, her elder, the dog who taught her how to move out of urban puppy position into teenager on the loose in the wilderness. They ran free in the forest and around our neighbor's pond with a mutual understanding of Rosie's superior knowledge.

But in Brooklyn, Dixie persecuted Rosie relentlessly. She chased her up and down the stairs, trapping her in corners, eating her food, and always snapping and growling. Even Molly understood the problems we would have trying to keep Rosie in the city.

"But," she said, eyes blazing, "even so, I'll never forgive you. Never."

We cheated her out of her pet; we violated the contract and, in doing so, we revealed our darkest hearts. But I learned one important thing from Rosie's fate. Never name a pet Rosebud.

You can see why I thought that a stray cat would fill up some of the emptiness and soothe away some of the ache. And as we watched

Welly tumble around the kitchen floor in pursuit of his tail, we could almost forget the nightmarish final days of moving out of Brooklyn.

Moving, we filled ninety-two green plastic garbage bags with the discarded pieces of our lives. Bags and more bags waited on the front yard for the dumpster. Two hours later, at around noon, the first scavengers arrived—Russians from the apartment buildings down East 17th. Three little kids and one old man stood sullenly beneath our window, all four carrying knives. With somber deliberation, they slashed open garbage bags to search through the contents. Pieces of Fischer-Price Toys, broken down paperbacks, moth-eaten school blazers from England, worn out panty hose, outgrown blue jeans, ten years of PMLA, dirty towels full of holes and more broken toys began filling up the lawn.

I ran out to chase them away. We bagged up the remains and went back inside to call the scavenger company about our Dumpster. No answer, but outside, the Russians were back, along with five Indian kids and a woman in a sari.

The children began ripping up the bags and jumping on the mattress from the spare bed on the third floor. The old man and the woman in the sari silently stared at the bags.

Denny ran out this time, shouting. In two days every one of the ninety-two bags was disemboweled. Each bag, gaping, grinning, reproached us for our bourgeois excess. How could one family waste so much? the crowd of scavengers seemed to ask. But then they would blunt the point by rejecting 95% of the discarded belongings. How could one family keep so much junk for so long? Either way we were guilty.

We finally gave up re-bagging entirely, and let the refuse fester on the lawn. No dumpster would come out to collect the junk over the long Memorial Day weekend, and the police began to warn us about citations. At one time, seventeen people stood on our small front lawn investigating tinker toys, old brassieres, and cracked pottery.

The scavengers were exclusively Russian and Indian. The African American kids rode up and down the street on their bicycles laughing, proclaiming to the world that they wouldn't touch that shit with a ten foot pole. The children of the white middle class, looking grave, were careful to avoid our side of the street.

Some of their parents called up to complain about the mess. "Was I aware," they would ask?

"Of what," I would yell back and slam down the phone.

Three days after the dumpster arrived, I was still finding pieces of us scattered throughout the neighborhood. Denny's boxer shorts, Molly's old knee socks, my shredded panty hose and Patrick's Cub Scout cap waving jauntily from the branches of trees two or three blocks from home.

Of course a cat like Welly was the perfect remedy. Welly would cure us all and make the hurt go away. During that first difficult year when I commuted between Boston and New York, from September1978 to June 1979, a cat like Welly would provide companionship for my orphaned children, giving them something to stroke while they sat in front of the VCR.

"Oh yes, of course," I said when Molly carried him home, holding him tight around his straining belly.

I think that if Molly had brought home a stray elephant, I would have found room for it somewhere. We had, you see, a deep basement and a large, fenced back yard. It might have held a small gray pachyderm swaying across the lawn, ears flapping, tusks shining, aiming her trunk over the stockade fence to spray the motorists lining up on Carlton for the long stop light. Or a black and white kitten curled up into a pulsating ball, breathing lightly.

Whether or not he was aware of the fantasies of domesticity we had projected onto him, Welly refused to comply. To be fair to this victim of our desires, I need to say that the dog persecuted him mightily. Without even a warning growl, she would lunge at Welly with bared teeth. Dixie was particularly territorial about her food. If Welly were one room away from a bone or scrap that she was guarding, the dog would thrash and roar, driving the cat out into the back yard and sometimes over the fence.

The cat would retaliate on Dixie's daily walks. That's when Dixie missed the country most of all, where walks were what she did naturally. Without a leash. Once she took off after a white-tailed deer. We found her two hours later wandering around in a swamp, grinning. Since she could never run free in Brooklyn, Dixie went into a Zen mode there, content to hunker down and wait for the weekends to run wild in the country. But when we left Brooklyn and Newfoundland for good, she had nowhere to let off steam.

She lived in Brookline all of the time, weekdays and weekends, always on leash. In Brookline, she was forced to submit to the indignities of her position as dog being taken for a walk, dog trotting obediently at the heels of her master and, as a dog, kept from her right to sniff and explore. Denny and I used to argue about the need for a leash. He was convinced that unleashed, she would throw herself into oncoming cars or run amok, sinking her teeth into nearby spaniels. Their aged owners would sue us for their pains. We'd lose our house.

There is no doubt that, on a leash, Dixie was losing her freedom. The cat, being wise in the ways of domestic combat, took advantage of his enemy's weakened position. He tortured her. He accompanied her on the most trivial walk, taunting her with demonstrations of unfettered feline independence.

Sometimes he would hide behind the fence, crouched, then leap into the air and land before a perpetually startled Dixie straining at her leash. Sometimes he would race a block ahead to loiter just beyond the church. The Hebrew School was a favorite ambush site. He would lurk under the cars in the lot and then run, bouncing off Dixie's side in his eagerness to show himself at last.

But always, no matter how he met Dixie on her walks, he always left her the same way—with bravado. Peeling off one block before they reached the house, zigzagging crazily back and forth down Monmouth, he would disappear triumphantly into the park next to the Brookline Art Center. His tail would brush against the sign prohibiting dogs.

"Oh," people would say, watching Welly walk the dog. "They must be such good friends. You're so lucky."

Welly became an outdoor cat of great prowess, mighty hunter of the rats that lived in the Muddy River, even mightier lover filling the night with cries of desire. We ignored the veterinarian's lectures on the dangers of feline sexuality. Nazis, I muttered, not having learned one thing from the pig debacle.

Our cat ran wild and free through the back streets behind Beacon Street where he battled fiercely with his amatory rivals. He also ran wild and free in the house, where he leapt from the mantel to the scratched table top to land on the shredded chair.

When he wasn't fighting his rivals or harassing the dog, he was scrapping with one of us. Welly was particularly fond of vaulting up to grab onto a wayward finger with his bared incisors. He wouldn't crunch down, and never broke flesh, but played with our appendages as if we were stunned birds. I must have encouraged him while I played tug of war with his clenched teeth, feeling his tongue slither roughly against my entrapped index finger.

But we were all chewing on each other then. Welly fit in too welly; Welly fit in too well.

It is now time to tell the history of my scratched corneas. The saga is short, but significant: one swipe from Dixie and one from Welly. Dixie's attack taught me how to deal with a scratched cornea. The lesson came in handy three months later when Welly injured my eye. But it was only after Welly bit my foot, and after Dixie and Welly scratched my cornea, that I paid attention to what the animals were telling me. They were trying, I think, to make me see.

Dixie scratched my cornea the first time during that terrible summer we moved to Brookline. The Pocono house was up for sale, emptied finally of pigs and chickens, cats and goats and ducks, freed perhaps from our own restless spirits. Bob helped me look after the move, barely speaking to me while we went over the place one last time. Wilbur groaned out back, waiting for us, Bob said.

"He'll be disappointed," he went on, "without little Molly to scratch behind his ears," but before he could describe Rosie's grief,

71

Jessie's fury, and Snowflake's depression, I cut him short. "It's over," I told him, angry but also ashamed, haunted that last night by the animals, the living and the dead.

The house in Brookline was too quiet. No chickens taunting the roosters, no piggy snorts, no ducks muttering from the rooftop. Just us—driven by silent fury, determined to make sense of one more move that was threatening to destroy whatever resilience we had left.

Denny was working for his new boss non-stop, strategizing in his sleep, while I was spending twelve hours a day in front of the computer banging out material on Swift and the body. We didn't even have time to fight. Patrick, still pale and skinny, was at Camp Kinderland learning about the holocaust and wheezing and sneezing and dying of mold. But, he insisted, it was still better than being at home. Molly, tanned and golden, a head taller than me, was at Camp Regis—hotel camp Patrick called it. He preferred the Spartan integrity of his Yiddish socialist enclave to the blandishment of sailboats on Lake Saranac.

Denny and I were getting ready for the seven-hour drive through the Adirondacks to bring Molly back home to Brookline. It would be, in fact, her first time at "home," for we had moved into the Brookline house after she left Brooklyn for camp.

The morning of the drive, I lay in bed half asleep, dreading the hours ahead in the car. We were barely talking to each other, hiding behind our mountains of printed materials. Seven hours of empty space to fill. Denny could fiddle with the radio dial looking for Merle Haggard and Johnny Cash, but what could we say to each other?

Dixie stretched out between Denny and me, her long, sinuous, strongly-muscled backside thrusting against my shoulder. She was licking Denny's neck while trying to push me out of bed. Suddenly, she twisted around to flick a paw at my face and barely grazed my eye. I blinked, surprised and irritated, dragged myself into the bathroom to flush my eye out with water, and forgot all about the incident. I was busy those days forgetting most incidents.

On our way home from Lake Saranac, my eye began to water. It flamed up, turning angry red, and by the time we reached Brookline it throbbed with a searing, stabbing pain. Denny drove me to the emergency ward at Mass General Eye and Ear, and left me there with Molly.

"Too much work at home," he said, "I got to get going. Call me when you're through."

The waiting room heaved with apprehension and despair. One girl was crying because she was going blind, an older woman had to be led to her chair by a sad looking young man, and over in the corner a large black man, his bandaged eye dripping blood, sang softly to himself. There were many cataract patients, clearly regulars, most of them arguing about their medications with their children and doctors.

I sat, holding on to Molly's hand, Molly unexpectedly tender. She sat still in the frigid air conditioning, shivering in her camp shorts and tee shirt.

The doctors and nurses spent almost an hour on my eye. They poked it and prodded it, flushed it out with various fluids, dilated it with drops, and examined it under a fluorescent light. The tiniest hair line scratch emerged, will you look at that, it's barely visible, they exulted, proud of their sensitive machinery and their quick bright eyes. They irrigated mine once more, warned me that the dilated pupil would be sensitive to light, even under a patch, applied drops to the quivering organ that by now felt the size of my skull, and slapped a patch over half of my face.

The patch destroyed my sense of balance. At first I tried to wander up and down Beacon Street, but quickly retreated back to the house. The sidewalk kept buckling beneath my feet, and I couldn't stand seeing the shocked faces of passersby. They reproached me with their undisguised curiosity. I seemed to suggest, somehow, those things that could go terribly wrong; I represented, in my infirmity, the dangerous side of a middle class life that should be perfectly safe.

One hot day, I was sitting on the sofa in the back room watching *Sunset Boulevard* on the VCR and drinking a beer. A neighbor boy who had finished mowing the lawn came to the door to be paid. He stared at me in horror and backed off, almost tripping himself in his eagerness to get away.

"It's okay," he stammered, "I'll come back another day when you're better," and he ran home to his mother, no doubt a better woman than I, the kind of woman who would never wear an eye patch, and would never drink beer in the day while watching Gloria Swanson bare her teeth and roll her eyes.

He reminded me, in his flight, of the fragility of my place. How easily I could become lost altogether. Only the pain oriented me, reminding me exactly where I was, at the still center of my enraged, pulsating eye. For the first four days, I huddled in the darkest corners of the house. Stray beams of light could penetrate the patch, probing deep into my skull.

I stopped working on Swift, unable to focus on the word processed words I was trying to write, but also unwilling to enter into his own ailments. He suffered from what he called "giddiness." He attributed it to eating 100 golden pippin apples one Sunday afternoon. He really had Meniere's syndrome, a crippling imbalance of the inner ear. I did not want to work on his loss of balance those days.

The cornea finally healed and somehow another year of intense dislocation passed. I commuted between New York and Boston, always worried about losing tenure, or more practically, worried about losing my purse, my keys, my kids, my mind, terrified of losing myself completely on the nine p.m. shuttle that I so frequently almost missed. I thought about writing a novel. I'd name it "Shuttlecock." But I never got past the title.

In April, I knew I was having a heart attack and paid $75 for another EKG, but I was found to be merely "anxious" and harder to lose than the pigs. Suddenly it was summer again, a tentative time.

I had decided to leave NYU, even though I got the tenure I'd killed myself for, to teach at Tufts. It would be better for the kids, we all agreed. I hated the change. No more commuting, but also, no more New York.

Boston seemed like a toy town. Chinatown extended, three blocks, the North End was a smidgen bigger. And where was downtown anyway? The kids agreed. We were trapped by the shrinking parameters of our new life. They didn't say that. They said that it sucked.

By the end of the summer, it all seemed too hard. I had ossified, no longer pliable and elastic. Denny and I had been to Cape Breton to try to heal things up. The lobsters were nice, but we were not. And then, two weeks before school would start, Welly scratched my cornea.

It happened one morning while I was scraping the tuna and egg cat food out of its tin. Welly, slowly, deliberately, reached up and swiped at my eye. I could feel his sharp, extended claw slice across the eyeball. He seemed pleased, turned quickly, and leapt down from the kitchen counter to run out the door. Almost as quickly, I followed, running out the door and down the street to the HMO.

"It's an emergency," I said, "I have a scratched cornea and I want it treated immediately."

The attendant looked at me hard, and said "You don't look like you have an eye problem."

I argued the point, bringing in my vast knowledge of the eye and how it hurts. The scratch would take a few days to reveal itself, but by then *it would be too late*. Most unwillingly, the receptionist directed me to the ophthalmologist's waiting room, where I harassed the nurses, trying to make them see that every minute my eye was untreated would mean ten more minutes of pain later. Grudgingly an intern dilated my pupil and examined me under the fluorescent light.

I tried to disguise my sense of triumph when he announced that the cornea was indeed scratched. But the nurse stared at me hard, and I realized that I had given too much away. Just how much investment did I have in my knowledge of pain?

The intern suggested that I seek professional counseling at the mental health section of the HMO. I accepted the card he gave me, but I didn't keep it.

This time, I only wore the patch three days; this time, the pain could be contained. I was getting good at this game, and yes, the intern was probably right. This sort of game was not one worth winning.

The cat bit my foot in the summer of 1986. Leaving NYU had been moderately successful. Instead of arriving home on the shuttle to an angry house of complaints, three days of grudges piled up on the doorstep, I was in place, the angel in the house moored uneasily at Tufts, making all things safe. And, in truth, because I was teaching just across town, there were some improvements.

Molly and Patrick had found friends and no longer spent five hours at a time staring at MTV. But my uninterrupted presence provoked outbursts of anger and frustration.

Denny and I fought. We fought out of years of differences grown lethal; we fought out of habit; we fought out of boredom. The dog would bark, and the cat would scratch, but they could not stop us from our pointless, titanic struggles.

I reckon that in two years we broke fourteen plates, ten bowls, thirteen wine glasses and seven coffee mugs. By then we were shaking up the outside world as well. The giant elm on Carlton was struck by lightning and, that February, one icy night, a late model Buick crashed through our stockade fence, knocking down the mountain ash we had planted the year before.

That was also the year that Patrick broke his right thumb twice, once in September and once again the following June, both times by falling off his bike.

Into this maelstrom came Tom, my brother, four years younger than me, Kat, his wife, ten years younger than Tom, and John, their son, who was then two. The ages are important. I kept seeing in Kat my younger self, full of hope, for she was pregnant then with their second son who would be Joe. (Emmett would follow three years later.) She glowed with optimism and a resilience that could not even be wilted by the heat wave that shimmered in the night. We sat on the deck drinking ice water and beer and telling old stories.

I'm close to my brother. He has, I like to think, almost forgiven me for my asthma, he has almost forgiven me for being the first-born. He has even forgiven me for tying him up, drawing Nazi signs all over his body with my mother's lipstick and locking him in the closet.

It was good to be with him that night, and with Kat, to talk about his newspaper and the gory crimes he reported. Patrick kept asking him about blood, how it glows in the dark, even when it's been washed off the walls. "Impossible? Is it really impossible to disguise?" he would ask. He was enthralled with the macabre context of Tom's writing life.

Kat paid special attention to Molly, trying to find out about what was going on in her adolescent brain, the one underneath her big hair. She even admired Molly's startling new eyes lined with black smudgy kohl. I loved seeing them together, Kat teasing Molly about her truant ways, and Molly unfolding, making herself vulnerable.

But however close I felt to them both that night, I was also closed. My unhappiness lay in my gut, the size of a clenched fist. Every muscle in my body was in spasm that night, even the ones in my toes, but I wouldn't let go of my creaking routine of bad jokes that baldly disguised the real craziness of my life. I was the older sister, after all, with an image to protect. I was wise, then, wise cracking, cracking up.

Denny wasn't on the deck that night. By then he preferred spending time upstairs in his air conditioned study listening to C&W, working on our taxes or cleaning his guns, far better occupations than the pointless effort of hot, lazy, late-night conversation. Dixie would be with him, lying at his feet.

I remember being glad that the dog was not around. She had gone after John two times that day, baring her teeth, growling, and once lunging for him. John talked about her on the phone for years.

"Do you still have that big dog," he'd ask, "you know, the mean one, the really big, mean one?"

We decided to make sure that Dixie would not be able to get into the back room where Tom and Kat and John would be sleeping. To secure that space, we carefully closed all of the doors leading from the front hallway into the back hall, kitchen, and living room. And we went to bed.

Welly was out at the time, making his nightly rounds. I used to think that he spent each night on the street in pursuit of the calico cat that lived four doors down. For such a little cat, Welly appeared tough and doughty, and would frequently swagger into the house resplendent in the morning light, never more than ruffled from the battles I could hear in the night.

When we later learned that he was leading a double life, purring and licking the gentle hands of an elderly couple six doors down that knew him as Midnight, I started revising my old myths. Perhaps he'd just been searching for peace, a place to curl up unmolested by our anger. All I know is that Welly left us every night with an eager swish of his magnificent tail.

By then, nobody but me had any use for Welly. His scratches and bites were universally and most bitterly resented. Molly had long ago dismissed him with contempt as a beast truly "welly." Patrick had been more actively engaged with the cat's neurotic attacks, recognizing in the biting and scratching a justifiable complaint being made against the entire household. But he too turned hostile after the ungrateful animal pounced upon him during the night and shit on his pillow. "Turd," Patrick shouted, threatening mayhem, "Turd, Turd, Turd."

I remained his champion. I liked him for waging openly the war that was raging within the family. My devotion was skewed of course; the cat never laid a claw on Denny. Nonetheless, his impersonal violence acted out the anger within us all. And when aggrieved family members threatened to throw him out the window for his crimes, I would resort to clichés, heartfelt as all clichés are, in his defense.

"Over my dead body," I would hiss, imagining myself a cat on a roof so hot that even in my heavy clumsiness I could fly free from its scalding surface of tin.

I let Welly in the front door at his usual time, seven a.m., and picked up the morning papers. The cat stood ominously still, staring in desperation at the closed doors to the living room, kitchen, and back hall. Before I could open a door to let him into the kitchen, where his food would be waiting, he leapt into the air, gave out a terrible scream, and dove for my bare left foot. He grabbed my instep with his front claws, and with one quick thrust came down hard on my flesh with his sharp incisors, leaving two bloodless puncture wounds. I was shocked more than hurt then. Welly mewed pathetically, and began rubbing my leg with his head.

"You're not going to believe this," I told my brother, and rubbing the holes with Listerine, feeding the dog and cat, grinding the coffee, I began the day in the usual way, domesticating the disasters.

Later that morning we drove over to Cambridge to wander around Harvard Square. I started to limp, and when we arrived at the Harvest Restaurant for lunch I was happy to sit down. My foot was throbbing by the time I got home, but I didn't want to take the time to go over to the HMO.

Who needed another computerized item on my medical record? "Second cat accident," it would announce, "mental health examination imminent."

My foot would stop aching, I was certain, as soon as we got to the beach. We had a tiny weekend house in Newburyport that Tom and Kat would be using for the rest of the week. I was driving up with them for the night.

We reached Plum Island in the late afternoon, the best time. Hardly anyone was left on the beach, only a few dog walkers and a family making a fire down by the water. John went wild. "Fish, fish, fish," he kept crying, "water, water, water."

He ran back and forth touching the shore, harassing the family making the fire, peeling off into the dunes, and returning suddenly to careen in circles around us sitting there. He whooped and hollered and wriggled and rolled, spitting out sand, sucking on shells, and draping himself in the stinking seaweed lining the shore.

Tom and Kat took turns watching over his expeditions into the water. I sat nursing my foot. It was starting to swell and turn blue.

We sat for several hours waiting for the sun to set. Mostly we watched John chasing after the gulls. I worked hard to ignore my foot, but when John tried to bury it in the sand, I cried out with pain that could no longer be hidden.

Kat kept after me about seeing a doctor. I didn't know any doctors in Newburyport, I argued, and we certainly didn't want to drive back to Brookline. We were spending the night here, not there, you could see my logic, and my foot would be all right in the morning. Brookline meant the dog scaring John out of his wits, Brookline meant Denny; I wanted to stay far away from them both, I knew, but I couldn't explain that. I talked instead about getting some lobsters and corn.

I could barely make it back to the car. My foot was two times its size, aching all the time with a pain that became unbearable if I stepped down. I hopped awkwardly, holding on to Tom, trying to reassure John.

"I'm OK." I kept saying. "OK. Really. I'm fine. We're gonna get some lobsters."

The sun plopped suddenly down into the marshes to our left, bringing out the deer. "Doggy," said John, "doggy?"

We couldn't find any place open that sold live lobsters and, by now, the pain was making me sick to my stomach.

Tom looked at me hopelessly. "Okay, Carol, what do you want to do? We can eat anything, but first you need to see somebody about that foot."

It was now the size of a melon ready to burst. My bones seemed to have disappeared entirely, consumed by this bloated, dead looking appendage that had sprouted from the end of my ankle.

We drove to the hospital. Since I was still embarrassed about my scratched cornea, I was mildly gratified by the stir I created in the emergency ward.

"Cat bite," the nurses and doctor exulted, "and it's on the foot, the worst possible place to be bitten. Get her on the table quick, get that drip going, this is serious."

I learned later that a giant ginger cat bit my doctor on the foot fourteen years before.

"It's agony," he said, "but I don't have to tell you that, and it takes days to heal up, and if you don't respond to the antibiotics, you've got to be hospitalized, oh boy, let me tell you the infection goes right to your heart, and—you know what that means."

I lay on the gurney for two hours feeling the antibiotics drip into my soul. The nurse changed the bags of fluid four different times, explaining why I needed penicillin and sulfa. You could never be sure what diseases your cat picked up, the filthy beast.

"I'm a dog person myself. Of course you've got to neuter them," she said, jabbing my vein extra hard, "if you want to keep them in their place."

Behind a drawn curtain I could hear a man worrying over Lyme disease, which in 1986 had become the newest local threat.

"Well I've been depressed, see, and under the weather, and my job's not going so good, and you know I started to think about that time that me and my wife went picnicking down by Maudsley, and I just wondered. There's plenty of ticks there, down by that old swimming pool."

Down the hall an older woman was crying into her hands. Her husband had been brought in after me on a stretcher. I think he was having a heart attack.

The puckering bags were finally emptied out into my blood stream. My doctor returned smiling broadly. I was to take four pills four times a day without fail, and see my HMO no later than noon the following day. The nurse followed bearing pills and crutches.

"It's essential," the doctor said, "to stay off that foot. Don't walk anywhere at all, except to the bathroom. This is dead serious."

He seemed so excited, so zealous, remembering no doubt his own epic battle against the cat germs now battering my heart.

"See this line." He pointed to a thin red path leading from the puncture wounds to my ankle. "That's what has to be stopped."

His voice broke and he shook my hand.

"Good luck," he said, "and keep your eye on that line."

I was turning the experience into parody, so much more manageable than real life, but I was scared. Waiting for my brother to pick me up outside the Emergency Room, I could feel the crutch digging into my sweaty armpit, and I could also feel the cool night air blowing in from the sea.

There would be a storm later that night. I could see the stars swirling in and out of quick running clouds. That made me dizzy. I was losing my balance.

I imagined Tom getting lost and not showing up. I would stand outside the hospital forever, hunched over my crutches, while the fatal red line shot inexorably into my heart.

But of course he drove up at last, with salmon steaks from Shaw's supermarket, with wine and cheese from the shop across the mall.

I felt, for the moment, reprieved.

We stayed up very late, eating and drinking and talking. I remember telling Tom and Kat my carefully kept secrets, the story of my real unhappiness so long withheld from them. The confession didn't really amount to much. My drinking, my anger, my unfaithful spirit, none of this surprised them.

I still skirted around Denny's violence; I was too ashamed. I'd worked particularly hard being the successful sister, the one who ran away from home with no regrets. The cat bite had not entirely loosened my tongue.

Cat got your tongue, what did that mean, anyway? Did I want to die lying? Keeping mortal secrets up to the end? Lying was a habit I'd picked up from way back, trying to disguise my mother's hard love. Tom didn't like to talk about her rampages. In fact, he seemed to forget them altogether, suspecting it was all drama, just smoke and mirrors, something I made up to get attention. How could I even begin to talk about Denny?

The next morning, right before I left Newburyport, John threw up all over the rug. It turned out that he was coming down with the flu, but we figured then that he was overexcited from the hours on the beach. As I waved goodbye, he cried, beating his fists against Kat's leg. Rain pounded the windshield, reminding me of the drip the night before. I thought about the cat germs swimming in and out of my immune system.

"Take Brewer's yeast," the doctor had said the night before, "and yogurt. You like yogurt? These antibiotics will wipe out your natural bacteria. Ever had a yeast infection?"

Maybe, I thought, straining to stay on the gas pedal with my cramped right foot, maybe I would crash into a welcoming Jersey wall somewhere around Danvers; anything to avoid a yeast infection.

But I got home safely after stopping at the HMO to be checked over by my nurse practitioner, a goodhearted woman who was worried about me. She'd studied my chart.

"Listen," she said, "get rid of that cat. Cats can be terrific, I know, I have two. But you don't have to keep one that bites you. You're not obliged to hurt yourself."

She got me in my weak spot. Of course I was obliged to care for anybody who showed up on the doorstep. Stray children, stray cats, robbers with guns, rapists, and mass murderers, they all belonged to me. *This is a stick up*, they would say, help, they would say, and I would pull off my stockings and stick out my foot for them to gnaw on with their shiny, sharp teeth.

I spent twelve days on the sofa bed in the family room overlooking the back yard. We lived in a semi-detached federal period three story brick house. The owners before us had modernized the back entrance, turning the two low stories where the servant's quarters and pantry used to be into a high narrow airy space surrounded by glass windows. When you pulled out the sofa bed, the mattress took up the entire width of the room. To my left sat the television, to the right, the kitchen. The door to the back yard stood flush before the end of my bed. Luckily it opened outward.

I stretched my left foot up and over the top of the sofa. I had to keep my foot elevated at all times. The doctor and nurse practitioner were quite adamant on that point. Each day I visited them on my crutches, and each day they would lecture me on the fine points of recuperation. They suggested that I wasn't pulling my load. They would have to put me in the hospital on a drip, they warned, if I didn't start to heal up.

And yes, I got a yeast infection. I began to feel guilty about my lack of cooperation. "You're walking on it," they would say, not listening to my hot, frightened denials. Tap dancing on the ceiling; they'd found me out.

No, I did not walk on my foot. Even the thought of pressing down onto its taut tender ball made me uneasy. The foot had become an object of contemplation. It waved before me, mysteriously swollen, alien in shape and texture. I imagined how pulpy and squishy it would be inside, germs and sulfa sliding through tissues already overloaded. It felt hot to my touch, ready to burst, in contrast to the firm cool right foot that began to cramp up from over-attention.

I loathed the left foot, but I also adored it, its piggy toes poking aimlessly upward. It had no character; it had my character. I missed my veins, taut and blue, I missed the slender ridge of bone extending above my instep into my big toe. Even my anklebone had disappeared into the morass of bloated flesh. Only my toenails, as always cracked and long and dirty, remained constant.

I spent twelve days on the sofa bed in the family room thrusting my left foot up and over the top of the sofa, waiting for somebody to take care of me. My kids wandered in and out, mostly embarrassed. By now they were tired of my body and its discontents. Patrick suggested that I was committing suicide by installments, Patrick standing over me, his third broken right thumb encased in a fiberglass cast that extended over his elbow.

Molly had even less time for the problem. I was as welly as the cat, a looosaah, and she demonstrated her healthy distrust of both organisms.

"Alright," she'd yell. "I'll get it any minute now. Hold on, foh god's sake."

I would find myself yelling for a glass of water querulously, violently, imagining in that moment just what it would be like to be really old and needy. I would not live that long, I decided, and I would take everybody with me.

The back room was hot and still, those long summer days redolent of sweat and fear. Lying on my back so many hours awkwardly thrusting my left leg against the scratchy, worn away nub of the sofa bed, I opened myself up to fantasies baroque and masochistic, Turkish and infantile. I was working on harems at the time, the seraglio as container of sexual desire, *see my chapter on Roxana*, but I dreamt of my own enthrallment then, not so academic, recreating in my fantasies the most fundamental needs and desires.

I returned to my earliest memories of sensuality, when I could be nursed and stroked and bathed and spanked, and punished, above all punished for my naughty, unruly spirit. I would be good, I promised, but that was impossible. I had to be bad in those daydreams of maternal tyranny to make the contact, however degrading, however illusive, last.

The cat remained ambivalently loyal. He seemed to understand somehow that he was responsible and also at risk. He would leap onto the sofa bed, scurry towards me, and rub his head against my foot. Gently. He never hurt me, but the entire time I was feeling his furry skull against my instep, I was imagining his fangs digging into my brain.

My passivity in this transaction enraged the kids. They spent hours together comparing the most macabre ways of killing the cat nine times over. He would be microwaved, flushed down the toilet, dropped from an airplane, buried alive in the back yard, nailed to the kitchen wall, thrown into the dog pound, fed to the giant carp in the muddy river, tied to the T track, forced down the garbage disposal.

"Turd," Patrick would taunt.

"Welly," Molly would whisper, "your days are numbered."

The cat would fly to me for protection then, uncharacteristically humble, burrowing in behind the sofa bed pillow. I could hear him purring; feel him shaking the cushions with a fearful desire to make contact.

I don't remember now where Denny was. He could have been traveling then, out to Long Beach, down to Houston, or to the Cape, or he could have been upstairs.

I remember Peter coming by one day with his friend Randall. I sat on my sofa, my leg thrust upward. We talked about the Whiskey Rebellion and HUAC and F.O. Mathiesson and smoked a joint. It was the high point of the twelve days and I don't even like marijuana. If they had come by a second time I would have run off with them both to Mexico.

My parents, on the other hand, were going to Hawaii—not running away but being sent off with a flourish of trumpets and drums.

They were celebrating their fiftieth anniversary on July 18th. I had to heal before then so I could get back to Chicago to honor them—to, as my mother put it, "pay a tribute to their marriage."

But I was, you must see by now, the bad daughter, the one who promised much but delivered little, enshrined in pictures from high school where I looked like Julie Andrews.

I sat on my sofa, my left leg thrusting upward, realizing that if I did not make it back for their gala, I might as well never go home again. I could hobble there on my crutches, cat on my shoulder, holding my IV before me. *Most likely to succeed*, they voted me, Morgan Park High School class of 1963, not realizing then how obliquely I would specialize.

Most of those twelve days seem the same except for the time Patrick came home at seven in the morning. He had been out to the movies downtown, with Tim and Sid. They watched *Alien*, twice, and walked back to Brookline through the parks—the Commons, the Public Garden, even the strip running down Commonwealth Avenue, following Olmstead's Emerald Necklace towards the Riverway, to end up in Amory Park off Beacon Street. He vomited, he told me, into every garbage can he could find. He was even stopped once for disturbing the peace by a Brookline police who melted at the lilting sound of the lad's Irish name.

One druggie stopped him between pukes to ask him his source. "Hey man," he said, "you got drugs there, what kind, my man, what's going down?"

My son looked pale and green and skinny blinking there under the pale morning sun, as if he were being exposed beneath a particularly malevolent fluorescent light.

"I threw up," he said, "way too many times, into the bushes, behind park benches."

And he stood there, waiting for me to do something about it, about all of it. We couldn't spare any more parts, Patrick and I. One thumb broken over and over, one cornea scratched twice, one foot bitten. Expensively and awkwardly, we were making our point.

I healed, knitting unraveled flesh into a fabric rare and wonderful. I had my hair highlighted by Phyllis on Newbury Street for the fiftieth anniversary gala, and I bought a splendid white wool pleated skirt to go over my black silk camp shirt, covered over negligently by a lavender linen blazer, sleeves rolled up at the elbows, straight out of Miami Vice. White silk stockings disguised the still swollen discolored left foot, and if you didn't look too closely, you would never be able to detect the limp.

"Oh Carol," said my mother, "you're so casual about your clothes."

She pulled back my hair, hard, clearly itching for a bobby pin to ram into my recalcitrant skull.

"And can't you do something about your hair? Why do you always hide your pretty face?"

We arrived at the Martinique Restaurant ten minutes before a thunderstorm that shook the windows and scattered branches around the parking lot. I thought about Welly back in Brookline, and I wondered then if he was lost somewhere in the rain. A friend of Patrick's would be coming to the house twice a day to feed the animals and walk the dog while we were gone. But what if Welly escaped out the door, ready to pounce on Dixie during their walk? Or what if he just bolted?

And I was right to worry. For the cat finally ran away that weekend in July, escaping forever the palpable anger circulating throughout the house. Molly swore that she saw him months later, sauntering down the street, answering to the name of Midnight. This was a black cat who let himself be picked up and carried around the block by a sweet-faced elderly woman; this was a black cat who would never, never bite.

We worried more about the anniversary celebration than about Welly that night. Tom and I had written out speeches about mom and dad, but we worried about finding a way to deliver them over the din of knives and forks clattering and scraping against china. A happy din, punctuated by bursts of laughter rewarding old jokes retold. Tom looked nice in his tuxedo.

Most of the guests had also been married for fifty years. They danced and flirted and posed for pictures that emphasized their hardy enthusiasm and their flexibility. I had known many of these people all of my life, but I felt removed from them that night. Perhaps I was protecting myself from their demonstrations of happiness, their obvious talent for accommodation.

"The secret to a good marriage," I heard over and over on that crowded ballroom floor. They should put it to music. "The secret is giving 51%, 99%, 150%. Isn't that right, Carol," they asked?

I was one of them now, marching—no, limping—into my twentieth year of marriage.

The massive doses of antibiotics had wiped out more than cat germs. I felt drained of vital juices, frail and brittle. Only my foot possessed life, and it wasn't mine. I kept stroking it furtively under the table. Cousins drifted in and out of view. We admired each other's children and pretended that we hadn't aged a bit. All agreed that Denny's gray hair was distinguished; nobody mentioned that I had become mysteriously blonde.

As the ice cream melted into the wafers, we presented the trip to Hawaii to mom and dad. They looked happy that night, holding on to each other. As if they hadn't quarreled that very morning over the travel arrangements. My father wanted to save us money. That was the point of the trip, perhaps the point of his life. A room overlooking the elevator shaft would smell just as sweet as a room with a view of the ocean.

"After all," he insisted, "we won't spend that much time in the room anyway. We're off to see Hawaii, for god's sake, not to look at the four walls of a hotel room. It's your money, yours and Tom's. Keep it for your fiftieth anniversary. You know, we just want to make you happy."

And he wouldn't budge.

My mother gave us one of her looks saying we'd disappointed her once again. Familiar words were said and unsaid, the old threats resurrected that morning before the party and, now, the drums were rolling and the tribute was paid at last to their goodness, and I knew, looking out over that dance floor, that I would never get to Hawaii.

I would become instead a Cat Lady. Imagine twenty Welly cats strolling across the parquet floor, tails held high. Twenty Wellys wearing twenty tuxedos, every one of them so dapper and debonair. Strutting forth to dance the black bottom.

I would feed them all fresh tuna in silver bowls to commemorate our twenty-five years together.

For our fiftieth anniversary we would dine on soup of turtle ladled out of a grand gold tureen, and I would sing to them all beneath the moon, the moon, the moon, under a banyan tree. And they would never, not ever, bite my foot.

THE DOG WHO WAS DEAF

THE SPRING BEFORE WE MOVED TO BROOKLINE, we tried to breed Dixie with a prize stud dog bearing one of those chivalric names like Galahad or Percival.

Dixie would have none of it. Even after she was muzzled, held down and sedated, even then she managed to break the tie binding her to her hapless mate.

The breeder sounded angry on the phone, barely able to be heard over Dixie's forlorn howl. We were obliged to breed her twice to fulfill the conditions of our original contract, but he told us then, raising his voice even louder, that he, for one, wasn't going to press the matter.

"Some dogs," he said, "have their natural instincts washed right out of them."

I thought that he was missing the point. Dixie's sexual desires were intact, but over-refined. She wanted to breed with humans, specifically Denny, although all of us served her needs for stimulation. Bellies, she would groan, stretching her body languorously across the Turkish rug, thumping her back leg in ecstasy as one of us diligently scratched her tender groin.

Most nights she ended up in one of our beds, burrowing under the sheets, searching for some mythical bone long buried in the mattress.

She never spent an entire night in one spot, but would wander from room to room guarding us. She liked to lick our assorted arms and feet. Pad, pad, pad, I would hear her making her appointed rounds, sometimes stopping to give a sigh. Her life was so demanding, she seemed to say.

We usually repress for very good reasons the sexual connections between our pets and us, but this was difficult to do in Dixie's case. Her size alone unsettled sentimental rationalizations. She was not cute. She was a large, beautiful animal with a muscular, sinuous body weighing around one hundred pounds—one hundred pounds without her clothes, which is partly the point. Dogs, and I speak now of female dogs, bitches as they are called, offer up to us their anuses and their breasts for our inspection.

I am not suggesting that animals wear clothing to remedy this situation. Do not confuse me with those cranks in England who want to diaper the police horses in Green Park.

I first became conscious of the insistent sexuality of Dixie when she was a puppy. Certainly she was bred to please, to win medals for her energy, her control and her beauty. Japan's national treasure was renowned for guarding sacred temples, hunting elks, babysitting and catching fish in its strong, noble jaws.

For these virtues, the Akita had taken New York by storm. The breed was relatively new in the States. Its first immigrants were smuggled out of Japan by GIs returning after World War II. Its rarity created a small gene pool and an extraordinarily high price. When it wasn't busy guarding its domestic space, it became the perfect apartment animal, happy to endure long hours home alone, sleeping on the sofa, on the rug or on the bed.

Hungry for admiration, Akitas also liked to be taken on short strolls down Broadway, to be stroked often and carefully by enchanted passersby. So went the urban myth. The Marilyn Monroe of the Dog World, the Akita became so popular in the eighties that Dixie's birth kennel had to be closed down in the early nineties for wantonly inbreeding its gorgeous show dogs. Many of its victims suffered from hip dysplasia or deafness.

But we couldn't have imagined that when we were driving Dixie to Pennsylvania in 1983. Our puppy nestled into my lap, shuddering with delight at my every touch.

Full grown Akitas have ears that stand up high on their heads; those pricked ears and their curled up tails are their trademarks. A puppy's ears might bend over, but somewhere in its second or third month, they prick up stiff and erect, proud signifiers of their breeding and potency. An Akita with floppy ears disgraces its breed; it cannot be shown, cannot be bred, and can never hold its head up high in the streets of New York.

So you can imagine our concern when our puppy woke up one morning with one ear standing upright, the left, and one ear flopping over, the right.

"Tape it," the breeder said, "and call me in a couple of weeks if nothing happens."

I not only taped the ear, I shaped it, molding it upward in my hands while I sang to it martial tunes of discipline and glory. "Lucy," I would whisper (I called her Lucy then because I have always found the name Dixie provocative and embarrassing, reason enough for Denny to insist upon it) "Lucy, my darling, prick up your ear."

On our trips to the country, two and a half hours each way, cupping it into my palm, stretching it towards me, I would hotly massage the offending organ. My motions felt obscenely familiar, reminding me of passionate hand jobs I had applied in high school back seats so long ago.

I had come a long way, baby, turning into a feminist matron obsessively manipulating my puppy's ear for her own good. And my exercises worked for, in the third week, the right ear pricked up high and straight.

Now a dog's ear is no more of a sexual organ than its snuffling, curious, phallic-seeming nose. The sexual vibrations rocking the car back and forth on those long hot drives had been mine, surely, projected onto the body of my animal. In those massages, as she would many times after that, Dixie measured our desires, reflecting back to us just what we were missing. And that is probably why, that steamy August, 1987, right before we were finally getting divorced, we decided that we wanted to try to breed her one more time.

We sent her to Staten Island on the shuttle. The breeder would pick her up at LaGuardia.

"It'll be a cinch," he said. "You'll have her back home in no time."

There would be, however, no home to return to, for it was up for sale, priced to move, and Denny and I were looking for separate residences, *amicably*, we said, lying. But the effort was true. We were busy packing up our separate lives and bagging up the debris one last time.

The house was oddly silent without Dixie. After Welly ran away, it was just the four of us studiously not talking to each other except in nervous bursts. Denny stayed on the third floor. He told me he only wanted to take a few things that originally came from his boyhood home in Danville. And his file cabinets and his desk, and of course the gun vault and its contents.

Patrick and Molly seemed to want nothing. Molly hung out in Brookline with her friends up "Lahzzie," aka Lars Anderson Park— site of teen atrocities I didn't want to know about.

Patrick wandered the mean streets of Boston with Charles and Nick. Sometimes they walked all night into the early mornings. They wore Humphrey Bogart trench coats and hats, looking like death warmed over. When he got back home, no matter how late, he checked for his weapons hidden under his bed, the throwing stars, the knives and the crossbow. He was ready to defend us, he told me. We'd never have to worry again.

Violence slithered through the old house. Molly and her girl friends trashed her bedroom walls with graffiti, while down in the basement, Patrick and Tim sledgehammered a Bosch juicer to death. I closed the door to my study and drank, pretending to read, while Denny locked the door to his study. It was hard not to hear Hank Williams and George Jones complain about cheating hearts and no good women. I imagined him taking his guns out of his safe for one more thorough cleaning.

Our divorce was amicable, you see, as long as we stayed in our trenches, vigilant and wary.

When Dixie did become pregnant, we asked the breeder to keep her throughout the birth and the whelping. We had, we explained, nowhere to keep her. She'd go crazy during the move, as she had each time before, barking at the packing boxes and threatening to bite the movers on their legs.

That is all true, but closer to the bone is the revulsion her breeding inspired. I imagined Dixie taut and swollen, her womb filling up with puppies, her breasts filling up with milk, and I felt dead, empty and dry. I could hear her barking in dismay.

I felt like barking at the packing boxes. There had been too many moves. Three in Boston and Cambridge, that's before we got married. In fact, Denny wooed me by carrying my boxes up and down rickety stairs all over town. Seven moves in California, one where I was almost arrested by police investigating our hippy movers. Maybe it was their dilapidated van, maybe it was their name, "The Red Sea Movers," maybe it was me, hair down to my waist, ripped jeans, bare feet, clutching my unkempt kids.

The police called Denny where he worked to verify my identity, to assure them that I was not a marauding counter-culture robber ripping off innocent homeowners.

"You gotta understand, lady, it's nothing personal. We're protecting the public from crime. The moving scam, it's real," the cop said, hiding his eyes behind enormous blue-mirrored sunglasses. "You want some advice? Cut your hair and wear a bra if you don't want the hassle."

I took a deep breath and didn't call him a pig.

Two more moves in London, one to New York, one to Pennsylvania, one to Brookline, and one to a condo in Boston not close to being inhabitable.

The condo might not have been ready, but the puppy would redeem us. It was always understood that Denny would keep Dixie when we divorced and I would get one of her puppies. In my hubris, I still imagined a dog of my own, imprinted with my own desires. While I did not harbor any theories about the emancipating, liberating effects of divorce, I did carry around utopian visions of a free, gentle dog running serenely through the streets without a leash. Her sweet strength would prove me right, somehow, in the battle that had been my marriage. I would be justified.

The puppy arrived on the last shuttle out of New York sometime in September. Molly went with me to pick her up at the Eastern freight office. Patrick had already gone off to Columbia to begin his freshman year, complaining that he would be missing the best weeks of the puppy. He remembered Dixie's floppy ears. He wasn't, however, sorry to leave the construction site that was our new home.

"You know, Ma," he said fairly often, "it's not as if I ask for much. So my life is fucked up by my dysfunctional family, I can deal with that, but at least I could have a bedroom with *walls*."

Dysfunctional. I heard that word for the first time that year, February 1987, when I went to a therapist, finally, for the counseling that had been urged upon me years before. Dysfunctional. Who knew? It comforted me, somehow, to have a word that I could attach to my childhood, to my marriage, to my present state. Dysfunctional explained everything. The word was like a Get Out of Jail card. It meant that deep down nothing was my fault. The dysfunction made me do it.

I was glad that Molly sat next to me in the car on the way to the airport. I hate to drive at night, particularly by myself. By then, she was talking to me occasionally, usually about the new kitten, small talk indeed, but better than the silences punctuated by hysteria of the summer.

We had decided on a name—Roxie, a combination of Rosie and Dixie, but also a name strong enough to stand on its own. I told the kids about Roxana, Defoe's courtesan heroine, and their eyes glazed over. That always happened when I mentioned even the word *eighteenth*. I didn't even have to say *century*, that one word alone was enough to send them into yawning and blinking fits.

Roxie looked remarkably like Dixie when she was a puppy, the same fawn coloring, same black beauty spots, same chubby, squared-off body (Akita puppies look like tanks), and the same bear-like muzzled face. Her pricked up ears separated her from her mother. I was happy to see that I would not be responsible for their development.

She wagged her tail tentatively, cocking her head to one side. We watched her wobble across the freight office floor with grave delight. "I don't want that dog shitting in here," the man said, but then he laughed. Molly's face glowed, all the sullenness melted away. She looked very pretty that night, her blonde hair shining under the neon light.

Have I mentioned that my children are beautiful?

We drove home in the rain. Molly held the puppy to keep her warm and we wondered what the ginger kitten would do.

The ginger kitten had lived with us, our jester, our gymnast, our diversion, for two months now, grown sleek and agile. She balanced herself on the most perilous roof beams, scurrying over exposed floor joists, and jumping wildly over the whirring electrical saw. She would handle a dog quite easily.

Molly had brought her home one night dripping wet and bedraggled. She had found her in the alley, she said, mewing, starving, drowning. It was raining, we had to keep her, she'd die out there all on her own. Molly wanted to call her Stinky, and I countered with Alexandra until Patrick broke the tie with a brilliant alternative, Kitty. The name was embarrassing to announce at the cat hospital.

A week later Molly confessed that the kitten was one of her friend Melissa's, no doomed stray at all. She had sprayed her with the garden hose for that special effect of wretched homelessness. When I asked Molly why, she explained that she was protecting herself from my hard heart. "I knew you'd be a sucker for a sad story," she said, "as long as it seemed true."

At first the puppy didn't even notice the cat slinking along the sidewalls of the living room. She seemed far more interested in the great hole yawning in the middle of the floor, the place where the stairway was supposed to be. She staggered over to the deep well, jumped up expectantly, stared hard, and barked.

I remembered that Roxie had been raised in the kennel, confined to a small caged-in space with her mother and brother. The vastness of our living room seemed to overwhelm her. She wandered cautiously around the piled up furniture, sniffing and nudging and butting the book boxes, stopping to gnaw on the stack of two by fours.

The cat stalked her, hissing, eyes narrowed, claws growing sharp and taut, but still the dog paid her no mind.

Roxie headed now for the dining room, the cat following expectantly, waiting for the inevitable confrontation. The round oak table stopped Roxie in her tracks. She sat back on her haunches for a deep, long look, and then began to chew on the table legs' lion heads. When I pulled her away, she shook her sturdy body, and began to trot around the table, faster and faster, three, four, five times, running her private derby. All the while she raced, the cat watched her with cautious suspicion. This was some sort of trick. Dogs don't act this way.

After the sixth revolution, Roxie stopped as suddenly as she had begun, stuck out her backside, and shit with great precision and efficiency. Her cage must have been circular. The cat blinked, and unable to contain herself, charged the puppy, tail waving, hair rising. She threw herself directly onto Roxie's back. Roxie shook her off easily, wagged her tail, jumped back, and grinned. We were living in a cartoon.

The next day the breeder called, sounding a little embarrassed. "How's that dog, Carol? Some dog, right, ever see anything so pretty? And what a disposition? Not like Dixie. Between you and me, let me tell you, that bitch is mean. You should have seen her go after the puppies' food once they were weaned. I thought she'd kill them."

He paused. "Listen," he said. I waited. "Listen. The vet said she might have a neurological disorder. I don't know what that means, she seems fine to me, holds her head funny, that's all. Doctors look for too much trouble."

Neurological disorder. It fit.

Patrick, Molly and I had spent the summer in our new condo on Medfield Street, two blocks from the old house on Monmouth street, one block over the Boston line, trapped in a construction site that would never go away. Because I didn't like the spiral staircase joining the first floor to the basement, I hired an architect/carpenter to design a glorious stairway that indeed did, when it was finally completed, turn a dumpy condo into a place of elegance and design.

But we paid for my aspirations. The stairway was supposed to be finished July 15th. It wouldn't be done until March 7th the following year, but luckily I didn't know that in September.

I only knew that I had violated the condo laws, the building laws, and the moral laws of Boston; I had been inspected twenty-seven times over the summer for my sins. This site is closed down, one elderly civil servant informed me chewing on his stogie. I felt like a madam in a condemned brothel. I was paying a structural engineer $95 an hour to save my skin. Everything I owned was covered in a plaster dust that seeped out of the bookcases and scuttled across the refinished floor. And most of our belongings were packed up in boxes sitting ominously against the sheet rock. They leaned precariously against the stripped-away walls. I would learn about deep structure that summer.

I took Roxie to the vet the following day. "See the way she holds her head," he said, "see the way it wobbles back and forth. She's probably got a loose retina, and she's moving her eyes back and forth to achieve some sort of balance. She stares hard at objects to keep them in place."

There was nothing we could do to change the condition. "Just don't breed her," he warned. "The condition could be genetic."

The condition seemed minor, the dog dearer for this small handicap. All would be well. I remember carrying her home in the rain, pressing her close to me. Three separate times dog lovers stopped me, panting with admiration. She was extremely winsome then, cocking her head from one side to another, ears pricked jauntily upward, posing for a dog food commercial. Who cared if she couldn't see the camera clearly?

Three days later I drove to Salem in the rain to get divorced. Three centuries ago I could have been burned for my sins of infidelity and impiety, and now, magically, I was driving over wet, shiny concrete in the Volvo, warm and dry, safe from harm. I would not be burned, I would not be ducked, I would not even be pilloried.

Instead of a scarlet letter, I would receive my maroon-colored car, child support, no alimony, most of the furniture, all of the books, none of the country and western records (I still miss them) and half of the proceeds from the sale of the house on Monmouth Street.

The hearing was scheduled for 8:30. It was 7:30 when I turned off Route 128 onto the road into town. Stalled traffic slogged down the exit ramp, extending far into the gray, wet fog shrouding the town. In one half hour we had moved two tenths of a mile. What if I missed my divorce hearing?

I imagined the lawyers, charging $150.00 an hour, flanking Denny, all writing me off as incompetent and unreliable. The thought of Denny reassured me, for if I was stuck in the traffic jam, then so was he. That's when I craned my neck to look ahead and realized that Denny was providentially two cars ahead of me in the same line.

Five minutes later the car directly in front of me turned out of the line in an exasperated U turn. I was close enough to touch Denny with my bumper. I could see the back of his head so tight and rigid, and imagined him staring into the rain. I wanted to make contact with him, but couldn't bring myself to press down on the horn. Too tacky, I thought, and I waved instead, but he didn't seem to see me.

Another ten minutes passed while the rain hammered away at the cars. Pedestrians glided by, attached to umbrellas, mostly mothers on their way to the elementary school across the road. I watched their large sleepy bodies swaying in the rain, hanging over their small wriggling children, and I thought about Patrick and Molly, so tiny when we lived in London. I remembered their red shiny raincoats bouncing ahead of me in the perpetual downpour, and I started to cry.

Denny was standing over my window tapping on the glass. I rolled it down and looked up into his strained, ironic face.

"Nobody," he said, "nobody would ever believe this shit," and he was right.

This made-for-TV scene would end with the reunited couple driving off together into the rainy sunset, to throbbing strings synthesized somewhere off the set.

I pulled out of the traffic line, parked the car on the side of the road under a large, dripping oak tree, and joined him in his car. He showed me his new radar detector and played me his new tapes while I admired his new, flatter stomach. We chatted nervously for the next twenty minutes until we finally glided into the town center.

Probate Court was hard to find, hidden between more imposing, judicial structures, but we finally found ourselves on the second floor waiting for our lawyers who were also caught in traffic. The crowd milling around us surprised me. Before now this had been our private melodrama, but suddenly we were surrounded by a universal grief that seemed impersonal yet oddly unresolved.

Styles differed. Some couples appeared almost affectionately coy, while others refused to look at one another. Most of us fell somewhere in between, our whispering voices falling into uneasy silence. Across from us one couple was making its final, angry demands in sign language. He must have been deaf and mute; she, on the other hand, would interrupt their silent argument with bitter side comments to her lawyer and then return to the frantic, anguished signing.

Their dilemma reduced all of our arguments to parody, and condensed all of our tortuous discussions to simple statements. *No, no, no* we had finally signed to each other far into those nights of anger, *no, no, no, no more*. And now there would be an end to it. *Basta*.

Our lawyers arrived. Baffled by our amicable state, they both urged that we reconsider. We had, you see, committed the perfect divorce. They had never witnessed such flexibility, such solidarity, but then they did not understand our talent for public performance. The gloomy archives stretched out before us, repository of all the failed marriages gone before us, stuffed with crinkly, yellowed evidence of irreconcilable differences. Dickensian clerks were sitting precariously on high stools. Not a computer in sight.

The actual hearing began shakily. After a few minutes of paper shuffling, the judge suddenly recalled that he had not sworn us in. We had to begin all over again, stretching in the process a two-minute ritual into three and one half minutes.

And then it was over, the lawyers headed back to Boston, and Denny and I had coffee a block from the courthouse. We talked lazily about Roxie and Dixie and the Red Sox, we skirted nervously around the kids, and we drove back in his car to mine.

I followed him then to the highway, but somehow got lost. I can't even say for sure when he actually disappeared from view, but by then it was raining too hard and I was crying too hard to see anything very clearly

Two weeks later my lover spent the night in the condo for the first time. This was, you can imagine, another mistake. But first I need to explain his name, or rather its absence. It would be easier to make a name up. I could call him Joe or Charles, Hugo or Reginald. Calling him *my lover* borders on the satiric. It doesn't sound as bad as Mr. X, but not as good as Tom, Dick, or Harry.

And that's not fair, for he was always very good. It is important to understand his significance in spite of his shadowy, anonymous existence on the page. He didn't cause the divorce, but he helped make it happen. He helped free me to think of a life less Gothic.

The Gothic. I used to use that term with my therapist, but she didn't understand what I meant. Living in the Gothic, I'd try to explain, meant being trapped by the conventions of a romance that I was writing for myself, me, the heroine of my story.

The story depended upon the heroine's ability to endure suffering. And that was something I did well. You could say that I had majored in suffering all the way from kindergarten into graduate school, tutored by my mother until Denny took over the reins. In fact I got a Ph.D. in the subject, specializing in *Clarissa*, Samuel Richardson's novel about the sufferings of a rape victim. It's the longest novel in English literary history.

No doubt about it; I needed to stop living in the long-winded Gothic. Too many pages of too much suffering had lodged themselves in my heart and in my head.

But it was hard to get out. I'd been fighting with Denny for a divorce ever since we moved to Boston, arguing bitterly through the nights and getting nowhere, looking for permission to leave that I never really needed. The lover provided a way out.

After our affair was finished, friends called him *a transitional figure*. That was a phrase almost as popular as *dysfunctional* in those divorce-ridden days, and probably just as specious. He did provide me with safe transit, not just safe, but loving. And that's why I can't use his name. I've already used him enough.

And so, my lover spent an uneasy night in the condo and it was, of course, a terrible mistake. I was, I reasoned, officially free, in the clear. I had entered a stage of willful sincerity, deciding in my pain to make everybody acknowledge my truth, but as I look back on it now, I think I should have kept lying for Molly's sake, if not for appearance's sake. I had no appearance left—Denny had seen to that when he called everybody in our address books to report upon my marital crimes.

And even as I write this I still do not know how I could have done it any other way. But when I brought my lover into the condo, I was perceived to be declaring war on my kids. Patrick, at least, was in his dorm at Columbia, safely surrounding by walls. Molly, rubbed raw, was upstairs.

We were very nervous, carefully picking our way around the minefield. The rubble of my construction site neatly fit the shambles of my new life. We were surrounded by boxes of books, familiar symbol of the real life, the one unsullied by loss. *Be all you can be. Read*, the sign had proclaimed over the Walker Branch Library on 111th Street. I believed in that sign with an ardent pure devotion. Reading is still the best thing I know how to do.

Somehow we got through the long night, listening all the while for signs of discontent, for wails and moans from Molly's room overhead, for thunder and lightning, hail and eclipses, plague and famine sweeping us all into the Muddy River, through the fens, into the Charles and down into the sea. Around five in the morning I remember hearing odd noises, tramping and stomping and laughter outside my window. My room looked out onto a tiny fenced garden separating us from the parking lot. I thought about getting up to look after the dog sleeping on the back porch, but I curled back into my lover instead, pressing against his sweet, solid back, falling into a deeper sleep.

Later that morning around eight a.m., I climbed upstairs to check on the puppy. Our kitchen door opened onto a wooden porch that led down into the tiny garden. The door had a wrought iron grate that provided security from *them*. I had never seen or heard *them*, but my neighbors assured me that *they* invaded unlocked decks and preyed upon unsuspecting apartment dwellers. They had taken on a symbolic importance as significant as that of the giant rats that were supposed to crawl out of the Muddy River to devour our garbage.

We'd barricaded the puppy in the kitchen to keep her from peeing all over the house. Before going to bed, at the last moment, I slid open the glass partition to allow her to move between the kitchen and the porch through the night. (At this point she was still small enough to wriggle through the wrought iron bars.) Molly and I had decided that Roxie liked stretching out under the stars (we interpreted her dazed acceptance of her new surroundings as heartfelt approval) and that it would be wrong to coop her up inside.

That guilty morning, I stepped over the childproof gate jammed across the kitchen door frame, opened the iron door leading onto the porch, and looked down for the snug round sleeping form. Roxie liked to squeeze between the terra cotta pots lining the fence. She was nowhere.

I started to panic, but decided that she might have learned how to climb down the steep steps sometime in the night. I scrambled down into the garden, and found the wooden door leading out into the parking lot wide open. I thrashed around in the ivy and rhododendron, calling Roxie's name over and over. Outside, the parking lot was completely empty of life. No tank-like puppy. Nothing but rain swept concrete.

For the next hour I ran in circles up and down Medfield Street, up Park Drive, down into the Muddy River, crossing the Longwood T tracks leading up to Carlton, onto Monmouth, passing my old house several times over. It stood there sturdily, reproaching my carelessness. When you lived here, it said, you were protected from yourself. You didn't demolish load-bearing walls without permission, and you didn't lose puppies in the night.

The old house was being renovated by its new owners. Even as I walked by, somebody was carrying a load of wallpaper, the brand new paper with small, yellow-sprigged flowers that had covered over Molly's graffitied bedroom walls. It was headed for the dumpster in front of the bay window. Maybe the puppy was hiding there, waiting patiently for somebody more responsible to watch over her.

I headed up St. Mary's, turned right on Beacon, right again onto Park Drive, back onto Medfield, and ran back to my garden, realizing that I had left the back door wide open all the while I had been searching for Roxie, the dog who would save us from ourselves. I would lose my keys next, I thought, and then my wallet, and all of my identification. I'd be found wandering along the muddy river wet and filthy, wearing water lilies in my gray, scraggly hair, singing obscene lyrics to myself, mad Ophelia a little long in the tooth. I woke up Molly, reluctantly, and told her what happened.

All of her rage over the divorce, the move, the lover, erupted. I should have realized that the dog would run away, who wouldn't try to escape such a place? When I suggested that the sounds in the early morning were robbers, she only laughed. My fault, she said, if it weren't for me we wouldn't be living in this slum. It was all my fault, my fault.

While Molly cried, I called the police.

A kind-voiced woman took down my information. "That's the saddest thing I ever heard," she said, and advised me to call the animal shelters.

By now my lover had come upstairs, tentatively offering advice to stony-faced Molly. He suggested putting up signs. "Neurologically impaired Akita," they would say, "needs medical attention. Reward." That way, robbers expecting to be in the possession of an expensive pedigreed champion would learn that they had dognapped an animal worth approximately fifteen cents on the market.

Molly rejected the plan. "I don't even know what 'neurologically' means," she shouted. "Impaired. What the hell does *impaired* mean, huh?"

These would be the last words she said to him for nine long months, until he disappeared altogether. But she started making signs anyway. They said, "Dog lost, Akita Puppy, Needs Medical Attention. Reward."

I covered the posters over in saran wrap to protect them from the rain. While Molly set out to nail them to trees, I stayed home and waited for the phone to ring. The enormity of my ineptitude overwhelmed me. I kept not learning essential lessons, and I was beginning to feel scared. What if it all went like this forever? I had divorced Denny to achieve some sort of control over the chaos that we seemed compelled to create. But now, on my own, with the best of intentions, I seemed to be the source of all confusion. This freedom to self-destruct was not what I had in mind.

Molly returned home and slammed her bedroom door—a familiar sound. It was by now almost off its hinges. I sat in a chair in the living room and hugged my knees, waiting.

In less than an hour, the phone did ring. A man down the street had the dog.

He said that his son and a friend had found the puppy wandering around the parking lot at around seven a.m. They carried it off to the apartment building where he was caretaker, and he'd been playing with it ever since. "What a sweetheart," he said.

They planned to post signs in the neighborhood as soon as it stopped raining. Then one of the boys noticed Molly's sign on Monmouth. His story puzzled me, but when I met his son and friend, I believed it completely. No way could these sweet-faced teenaged boys be robbers in the night. I gave them each twenty dollars and held onto the puppy all the way home.

I never have figured out what happened that night. Sometimes I imagine drunken louts clambering up our staircase to release the dog into the parking lot. I do remember the sound of footsteps almost overhead, perhaps on the stairs leading onto the deck. It's particularly difficult for me to imagine how the puppy could push open the heavy wooden door leading onto the parking lot. I can see how she could have tumbled down the steep stairs. In fact, she seemed to retain a traumatic memory of some great fall.

For two long years, Roxie, no puppy, but full grown, ninety pounds of sinew and muscle, would not attempt to climb down any stairs anywhere unless she was on a leash.

"Yo Roxie," I would call, "Yo Roxie, come on down and play."

Eager as she was to comply, she would stop short at the top of the basement staircase and whine. Sitting on her haunches, her quivering snout pressed between the banister posts above the staircase, she would drool down onto the steps below, missing me terribly. It was cooler down in the basement where I wrote. She wanted to escape the ninety-degree heat and sit by my feet as I typed onto my computer, but she never could make herself walk down the stairs.

When we tried to entice her with liver treats, she cried, dropped her proud tail and backed away, her soft eyes pleading for understanding. Even the cat and her kittens could not seduce her into moving past her fears. They tumbled down the back porch stairs, cheekily escaping her attentions. She stared patiently down at them, drooling with desire, studying them just as she studied her jettisoned chewing toys lined up out of reach at the foot of the stairs. I loved her then, so patient, so stoic, accepting without frustration, such a crazy handicap, my Roxana.

It took us about eight weeks to realize that Roxie was stone deaf. "We" by then meant Molly and me. And Roxie made three. Four if you counted Mike, the builder, humming to himself off key as he painstakingly built our beautiful staircase.

He worked on the condo for nine months, perpetually surprised by the time and effort that everything took. Patrick was at Columbia, happy to escape the sound and fury of condo rehab. The lover stayed wisely away.

We were trapped together, Molly and me, in love and in disappointment, behind the flimsy walls under repair. Our voices floated up into the condo above us during our early morning fights. Operatic battles raged over the question of getting Molly to school. First it was the bed she would not get out of, and then the breakfast she refused to eat.

Two hours later she needed a ride to school. "It's way too late for the T," she'd yell. "Ma, you'll make me tardy again." An hour after that outburst she needed a note to excuse her from first period, sometimes the second period, sometimes the third.

We screamed at each other, trying for sotto voce, but failing miserably. Finally we'd break out into a chorus of *no no no, should should should, never never never*—in two wavering parts. The poor lawyers living above us banged on our ceiling, their floor, for peace and quiet.

Only Roxie remained still, undisturbed by the racket.

At first her dear indifference comforted our weary souls. We delighted in her serene and majestic tolerance of the yapping, snarling dogs that bounded up to her near the Muddy River.

See, I would crow, this dog is no snapping defensive bitch, no Dixie, teeth bared, taking on the rest of the animal kingdom. This dog, our little Zen master, transcended the petty annoyances of the more boisterous animals blocking her path.

But gradually, inexorably, the severe nature of her handicap could not be denied. Our Zen master was not transcending the snapping and snarling of her enemies. She was not hearing them. She slept right through our noisiest entrances. Bang, clang, we would be dragging the groceries up the back stairs, crashing into the kitchen, and she would continue to snore, sweetly dreaming of rabbits, her leg twitching in delight.

The vet confirmed our suspicions. He had only one piece of advice. Training, he warned, was almost impossible. "People will tell you otherwise," he said, "but basically dogs are trained by oral commands. Just remember one thing. Never, and I mean never, let that dog off the leash, not even for a minute. She'll take off after a squirrel, and you'll never see her again."

No long walks in the country, the dog tearing up and down the hills, tail waving before us, no utopian experiments along the muddy river or in the Arboretum where I could watch our dog domesticate the canine universe with her goodness, no freedom anywhere.

When they learned about Roxie's deafness, friends fell into different categories. Those cynics who knew my plans to raise a "free" Roxie appreciated the irony of her infirmity. The more earnest and stubborn insisted she was not really deaf. Snapping their fingers and jangling their keys, emitting bizarre shrieks and whistles between clenched teeth, they confused Roxie with their wild and erratic movements.

"Look," they would exult, pointing down to her startled brown eyes, "look at the way she stares up at me. She hears me; I know she does."

Snap, snap, clap, clap. These types would also leap down to clap their hands with enthusiasm behind her head. When she would understandably jerk around to follow their dislocated bodies, they would draw the usual conclusions. She can hear, they would crow. If I only had a more positive attitude, I'd be able to do something with this fine animal. It was my duty.

My more didactic friends granted me her deafness, but came bearing theories of animal training. Look at Helen Keller, they would argue, imagining me, for the moment, as Annie Sullivan. Most of their plans were based on the assumption of two things: her readiness to be trained and my appetite for discipline.

I was, you see, profoundly unsuited for such a task. Assuming authority bothered me. Blame it on my overly disciplined childhood, blame it on my generation, but discipline, as we said then, freaked me out. I read a book in defense of the well-trained pit bull, written by a philosopher at Yale who argued that only through discipline and work could there be freedom.

Counter-defensively, I made arguments against well-trained animals demonstrating their submission to a higher good. "Whenever I see a dog dancing on its hind legs for a cookie, I want to throttle its owner," I announced.

That might have been true, but at the same time, I also knew that I couldn't get a dog up on its hind legs if my life depended upon it.

To quiet my critics, I did buy one hour of discipline for $25 at the animal hospital. An overweight man with tattoos on both biceps (tattoos were rarer then, not signifying urban chic) jerked Roxie hard on her collar.

"Ya got to show her who's boss," he said; "it's her versus you, and you gotta win. Otherwise she's miserable, the bitch, the little shit, I call them that, you see, but I really love them, don't I, dog's breath?"

He was particularly bent on making Roxie lie down abjectly before him. He pressed down hard on her front paws with his huge feet.

"This is the sure-fire method," he said. "As long as you can get her into this position, you're the boss, all the rest will follow. No sweat."

I apologized to the dog all the way home, massaging her bruised front paws, so tender, her rough under pads throbbing in indignation.

No, I am not proud of my inability to train my deaf dog, not then, not now. Freedom through discipline: the thought is a heady one. Maybe I couldn't hurt her, or maybe I just didn't want to take the time to enter deep training, but I know that I couldn't press down on her front paws. Not when she looked up at me with such uncomprehending surprise.

Roxie took the time instead to train me, taking me in the process down the street and into the park on long crazy runs, walks, trots, she leading, I following, winding around the complex shores of the Muddy River.

The sweetest of my didactic friends was David. He took Roxie and me to Amory Park one raw winter day, his pocket bulging with crumbling dog treats. We walked Roxie into the sanctuary, a fenced in area around Hawes Pond, and took her off the leash. She seemed astonished by her freedom, as she careened off in several directions, chasing madly after birds hopping around the pond's edge, always in the end running back to us for reassurance.

David would reward her return with a biscuit which she wolfed down gratefully, but I suspect that she ran back to see us out of curiosity, out of conceit. *Can you see me,* she would pant? *Did you get a shot of me terrorizing that squirrel?*

Roxie never seemed too inspired by biscuits anyway, preferring to chew up more expensive artifacts like eyeglasses, wallets and retainers. But that day, in the fenced-in sanctuary, there was hope for Roxie to run free. I was the limited one then, not able to imagine extending David's training methods onto the outside world.

We stepped beyond the fence and kept her running between us, rewarded by the crumbly cookies, but all the while I knew that on my own I would never be able to let her off the leash. Each time she ran away from me I imagined her barreling past David into Amory Road to end up under the wheels of a car.

Instead of freeing her, I bought her a longer leash, an expandable German contraption of tough red plastic, $45.95. It extended forward and retracted from a pulley that allowed Roxie to run fifteen feet ahead in pursuit of birds, squirrels and bicycles. This gave her enough room to wade into the Muddy River and stand there grinning. Enough room for her to leap into the air after pigeons too slow and fat to get out of her way. Roxie would bend down, making herself very small, eyes glued to the pigeons four feet ahead. I like to think that she was happy in those moments she spent trying, so patiently, to catch a bird.

For some reason, she seemed to understand the importance of silence in these hunting expeditions. Her sophistication about sound—when to make noise and when be silent—complicated our ideas about her deafness. She knew how to bark to get my attention, but she also could bark out the window at what seemed to be nothing at all.

And when she lay flat on the floor almost asleep she rotated her ears radar fashion as if she could receive sounds that we could not hear. Creeping slowly forward, tail slinking behind her, ears flattened against her square head, she would suddenly lurch forward fifteen feet, as far as the leash would permit, and scatter the pigeons into the trees. I think that she thought that she made them fly.

The expandable leash could cause its own problems, particularly when Roxie wrapped herself around the prickly bushes that separated her from her target. Once in a particularly ardent rush, she tied me up to a tree so intricately that it took me a half hour to disentangle myself. Half way through the tedious process, I found myself being dragged into the muddy river, carried away by her strength. I was fifteen minutes late for school that day, bruised, scratched, embarrassed, covered for a change, not in plaster dust, but in mud.

The expandable leash caused many problems. Once a balding middle-aged man with a soft, puffy belly warned me that it was illegal. His own dog, a lean and jumpy Doberman, kept lunging towards Roxie, growling and frothing at the mouth. Roxie, overcome by some primeval social response, pulled so hard that she released the catch and began to run the full length of her leash towards the man and his dog.

"I'll call the police on you," the man shrieked, "there's a law against those leashes, you ought to be arrested."

Roxie drooled on his shoes, and then raised her head to observe with great solemnity his furious face.

Roxie did that a lot. She loved to stare up at people, willing them into submissive admiration. When she was particularly determined to make an impression, she would stubbornly sit back on her haunches, cock her head to one side, and grin benevolently. "Look at me," she crooned, "Notice my nobility, my carriage, my completeness." Joggers had no time for her nonsense, cyclists careened out of her path, but the gentler walkers succumbed to her determined charm.

She also stared down the Tai Chi people, breaking into their hard earned concentration with her own purposeful meditation. It was then that I appreciated her Japanese pedigree. There was a reason that our dog, not western at all, had been designated a National Treasure and a Royal Guard of the Temples and Palaces, in spite of her undignified drooling.

Roxie stared hard to hold the world in place. Stalking leaves and trees and birds, she acted out her desires voyeuristically, seeming to fix her prey with her eager eyes—however out of focus. Her passion for order gave our walks purpose and taught me, unexpectedly, patience.

One winter morning after the first hard snowfall, we passed by a snow woman. The sculpture possessed large round breasts, carried a cheap plastic handbag, and wore a red apron and a brown wig. The minute she spotted the snow creature, Roxie began to growl with uncharacteristic menace at this anomalous artifact, inorganic, yet vaguely human. It seemed to violate her notions of natural order. She turned tail, then, and whined, begging me to run away with her.

The next day she began to pull on the leash long before the snow woman came into view. Then she crept down low, yelping painfully as I dragged her, cringing, past her enemy.

After a warm spell, we passed the rapidly melting snow woman losing both its shape and its power. Roxie's tail rose high in the air as she sauntered negligently past the spot. The next day, she dragged me over to her vanquished fetish and bent down to lick the almost dissolved form.

She carried the handbag half way home, growling when I tried to remove it from her mouth. Finally, in triumph, she dropped the bag into the gutter. Since her illusion had melted away, the purse left behind was reduced to a powerless token. Why couldn't I do the same, I wondered? I hadn't even been able to open up all the moving boxes—the ones too full of loss.

Policemen on horses, roller skaters, and riders of wheelchairs and lawnmowers all struck terror into Roxie's soul. They did not fit the scheme of things. Statues could both thrill and threaten her, for there is a hard, crude joy in these encounters. She also barked at mannequins in store windows, bent on frightening them into submission.

But nothing thrilled her as much as a glimpse of her own terrifying reflection. She would attack her image glaring back at her from the sliding glass door; occasionally she waged war with the mirror in the hallway. One spring night, we passed by a large, flourishing garden in front of an apartment on Monmouth and Carlton. A life-sized black and white cutout photo of a scarecrow loomed over the plot, secured against the red brick wall. I was glad that she was on a leash. Even then, she knocked me over, struggling toward her rival.

Her terrible fascination with the anomalous led me into trouble one unusually warm Sunday morning in January. I was walking Roxie slowly along the Muddy River's edge, feeling the sun on my face. Spring seemed to be erupting all in a rush, the way it can in New England, thawing out my chilly caution.

It was not surprising on such a day to hear music. A man stretched out along the bank was playing a mouth harmonica. The instrument, around two feet long, covered much of his face. Hidden, he became part of the instrument, and from within it, he delivered discordant melodies in a minor key of haunting beauty.

Roxie stopped transfixed. She sat down to stare at the musician for a good five minutes. He appeared not to notice, but played on, producing alien, disturbing sounds that filled the park with wonder and menace. Of course Roxie couldn't hear the music, although I still wonder about the high notes. She was, I think, studying the enormous mouth organ that seemed to extrude from his face.

He stood about five and a half feet tall, couldn't have weighed more than 130 pounds, and seemed to be in his late forties. His thinning reddish brown hair and fuller beard matched his faded tweed jacket and trousers. He carried, I remember, a tan pack upon his back.

I finally pulled Roxie off her haunches. We made our way down the path, approaching the man very slowly. He rose, seemed to tip a non-existent hat, and continued to play. We edged even closer. Roxie was by this time entranced rather than frightened by his appearance. She started to smile and to wag her tail vigorously. He moved towards us and abruptly changed his tune, playing a discordant version of the tune from *The Twilight Zone*.

I stopped and stood still to listen, until suddenly the musician pushed against my body with his mouth organ.

"You're in trouble now," he shouted shrilly, "real trouble. This is against the law."

He blasted his instrument, and then resumed the tirade. "Take everything out of your pockets, everything, every last thing, I'm with the police."

I stared at him.

"I mean it, everything in your pockets, get out your license; I'm taking you in for disturbing the peace."

All the while he ranted, Roxie kept wagging her tail. She seemed to enjoy his gesticulations, his popping eyes, and his jumping, thrusting, hopping movements.

"Listen to me," he shrieked, "I'm not kidding, everything out of your pockets now."

Had I anything in my pockets, I might have complied, but since I carried only my keys, I yelled out "no fucking way" and began to run. The dog stood back, still wagging her tail until I dragged her after me and ran across the grass and onto the road out of the park.

I am not a fast runner, but the dog slowed me down even more, dragging behind for one last look at the mouth organ. At the edge of the park the musician stopped chasing me and started to play the theme from *Star Wars*, wildly off key. I tried to walk casually up the path towards Park Drive, as if nothing so awful had happened. Roxie turned back one more time, to stare at him in adoration.

Violence works in a funny way. It can often make me assume a calm, rational mask to hide the terror. That's how I was brought up, that's how I stayed married to Denny. Stay cool, I would tell myself. Run from it if you can. Roll with it if you must. But if that's impossible, never lose control. Deep down, if forced, I would stay frozen to the core. It seemed safer that way. Nobody would be able to see that I was shaking inside, not even the police. In fact, this time, they laughed at my story, and I let them.

When I dialed 911, the kind-voiced woman on the phone murmured that the story of my attack was the most frightening she had ever heard. Three cops, all young men, answered the call for help. They were all visibly unimpressed.

"Did he hurt you," they asked, "did he try to rape you?"

When I answered no, they lost interest.

"You're lucky," they said. "But you know you shouldn't even be walking around here. Things happen around here. Bad things. Do yourself a favor. Don't count on that dog taking care of you. He's a pedigreed, right, expensive, right? And just how did Mr. Rin Tin Tin defend you?"

All the while they insulted her, Roxie kept leaping up, trying to lick their ears and necks.

"Listen, lady. You should definitely not be hanging out on the Muddy River. I'd tell that to my own mother. It's too dangerous here in the city. You oughta move to Needham," the pimply-faced one said. "That's where my mother lives."

I wanted to bite him.

Roxie, I knew, would never protect me from the attacks of strangers in the night. She'd probably approach my enemies with her usual grace, panting and drooling, trying to leap with friendly abandon onto his or her shoulders. She might even sniff his or her crotch, for she is a bisexual lover of strangers, but she would never protect me. No, I did not expect to be saved by Roxie; it was my job to take care of her.

She was not her mother's daughter; she was mine. Dixie possessed such a territorial instinct that we often found her growling with menace in front of the broom closet. Once when Denny and I were gone for the weekend and my mother-in-law was watching the kids, Dixie came upon her in the middle of the night in our bed and patiently, deliberately removed all of the covers. Then she took my mother-in-law by the hand in her firm but gentle mouth to lead her out of the bedroom into the spare room upstairs where she belonged.

But then Dixie also bit Patrick when he was unfortunate enough to come between her and her bone and snapped frequently at Molly, once breaking the skin on her leg. Oh, I already knew that I did not need a guard dog like Dixie. It was easier for me to take care of myself, the kids and Roxie without one.

Meanwhile Roxie took care of the kittens. Growing up with their mother, she kept adjusting that first year to the way that they changed in size and in power. At first Roxie was as big as Kitty but pathetically unequal in dexterity and speed. The cat would dash around her, leap over her back, and finally pounce from across the room to land triumphantly onto her rump. Roxie then would roll over on her side to wrestle her mysteriously graceful adversary.

But as she grew bigger than Kitty, their relationship shifted to accommodate crucial differences. The cat could still run rings around Roxie, and, if they were very careful, they could roll over each other in mock-heroic demonstrations of their desire, but they both seemed to realize that one swipe from a thudding paw, or one careless bite, would end their game.

Up until the last day of her pregnancy, Kitty would stand up on her hind legs on the dining room chair to box and pummel Roxie on her nose. Roxie would sit patiently before her, raising a carefully guarded paw into the air to swipe symbolically at her partner, careful always not to touch her swelling stomach.

The day that Kitty gave birth, everything changed. Motherhood made the cat act as if she were on speed. She began to mew insistently and wander around in crazy circles. Suddenly she darted back and forth between the bedroom and the hallway. Her mewing stopped for about ten minutes, until suddenly, two separate shrieks, one strong, one feeble, came from the covered litter box next to my computer. And Kitty leapt out, covered in green pellets, to run into my bed. She tore off again and hid in the closet.

I listened in horror to the desperate noise coming from behind my gym shoes, and watched with paralyzed fascination as a contorted, slimy little body slid onto the floor. Its afterbirth followed somehow, and lay quivering before me.

At first I thought that the thing was an aborted fetus, but when it kept mewing, I realized that it was still alive. I dragged out a laundry basket, covered it with towels, picked up the shapeless kitten, and shoved it between layers of terry cloth. Kitty nudged my leg, quivering with fear. I picked her up, stroked her, and placed her next to the kitten. She cringed and hid from it, but the kitten bored into his mother's body demanding the right to be licked, to be fed.

I carried the basket up to Molly's room, and we watched the other kittens being born. By the sixth, Kitty knew what she was doing. She expertly licked off the afterbirth and bit off the cord before she settled into nursing. I could hear the dog panting outside the door. I knew that she would be sitting there, legs curled up beneath her, imitating in her posture and in her patience, the cat.

Roxie spent many hours waiting. The cat carried her children into Molly's closet where she nursed them and licked them with desperate devotion. Motherhood seemed to consume her. Driven by a perpetual compulsion to answer each kitten's demands, she rushed from one mewing creature to another, never seeming to sleep or eat. Every few hours she would straggle out of the closet, her fur disheveled, her eyes dull, to flop near Molly's bed.

The dog, panting with enthusiasm, would lope over to Kitty, eager to continue their friendly battles, but she would roll away from Roxie in hostile irritation. Roxie could not hear her hissing, but she did seem to understand the meaning of the cat's outstretched claws. Roxie would back off then and fall to the floor with gingerly caution, her confused head held sullenly between her outstretched paws.

She reminded me of Wilbur then, another animal trumped by motherhood, waiting to be let in.

It always surprised me that Roxie never followed the cat into the closet. I realized that she couldn't hear the muffled signals coming out from the depths of Molly's dirty clothes, but I would have thought that the dog would have been able to smell out the litter. Perhaps she obeyed a higher law of restraint. Simply and patiently, she waited outstretched in front of the closet door for the kittens to come to her.

One day I came home from school to find Rox surrounded by six fuzzy, half-blind kittens, all of them tumbling and staggering around her great body. The cat must have carried them out to show them to Roxie who was lying there in ecstasy. She panted and drooled and smiled and sighed and stared in wonder. She'd never looked so happy. When the gray kitten rolled against her paw. Roxie nudged it with her nose and covered it in saliva, but made no larger gesture. Kitty watched her cautiously.

As the kittens grew, Roxie's attentions expanded. She tried to walk around the kittens, but usually failed. In her clumsy bulk, she was a gigantic alien being who could send them scattering into the closet to burrow under the clothes. Like Gulliver awkwardly finding his place among the Lilliputians, Rox kept trying to pick the kittens up in her soft gentle mouth. Freed from her jaws, drenched with her love, they would tear away from her, teaching her with their vigorous rejection what not to do. They preferred to make the advances in their play.

Once I saw all six of them circle around her to pounce in synchronized grace onto her stomach. Roxie shuddered with delight. The calico cat named Pandora liked to charge her nose, while the black cat named Mouse became fond of gnawing on her tail. I think that Roxie imagined herself to be their mother, the true one who would answer their deepest needs.

Realizing that we could never breed a deaf dog, we had her spayed in her sixth month, around the time that she would have gone into her first heat. She began shortly after the operation to play solemnly and deliberately with Molly's stuffed animals. She would collect the stuffed animals together and line them up on the couch and offer them chewing toys and bits of debris in tribute. Then she would carry them, one-by-one, out onto the porch to continue her nursing.

These sessions usually ended dramatically when she would take them to the top of the stairs and drop them down. I used to think then that Roxie was demonstrating her highest intelligence. These things weren't flesh and blood. Real children would spurt blood as they crashed against the ground below. Stuffed animals just thud pleasantly to grin up at their mother. Thump, thump, we heard—a sound that Roxie could only imagine.

One morning, I heard a terrible thrashing from the front hall. Roxie was standing over the cat's box, busy at work trying to bury a bone in the fresh kitty litter.

She never objected to sharing her food with the kittens. She stood by in bemused, generous contemplation while they edged around her enormous bowl. And they were truly a sight to behold teetering crazily as they tried to make a dent in Roxie's mountain of chopped beef. She even let them nibble on her bones and chewing toys, allowing them more freedom more than she ever offered to their mother. *Choose me*, she seemed to say, even as she frightened them away, her tongue dripping with desire. *I will shower you with riches.*

Roxie was not alone in her desire to be chosen. We were all making promises then, all in the name of love. *Choose me*, Molly cried, reminding me, how much I needed to take care of her. Patrick was more subtle. He demanded space rather than love. I understood how it was easier to love us long-distance. Easier to avoid feeding the flames of resistance that Molly and I kept stirring up at home. At Columbia, he could engage in his own life and create and solve his own problems.

And he had his problems. New York was so much so much bigger than Boston, filled with so many more challenges. Fires even broke out there on the fifth floor of his dorm. I remember walking skittishly around a charred and smoldering heap in the middle of his hallway. Notebooks, Patrick told me, sacrificed to the god of final exams.

"Not to worry, Maa," he said. Somehow, I didn't. The riotous celebration had a generosity about it that was missing from our own domestic life.

Choose me, demanded my mother querulously from Chicago, in long-distance reminders of my failure. She had become so angry about my indecent behavior that she refused to "inform," her word, even one friend or relative about my divorce. I had shamed her for the last time. Why, she asked, should she publicize her failure as the mother of such a reprobate? It was time for me to settle down and mend my ways.

Choose me, cajoled my father, giving me permission to phone my aunts and uncles and cousins and second cousins to tell them about my divorce. But I would need to swear them to secrecy. He would never forgive me if my mother learned that the relatives knew about my shameful state.

As long as I was changing my status, I could drop my married name, Flynn, and also lose my maiden name, Houlihan. And why not, he asked, why not throw out Carol while I was at it? Then I could take his mother's maiden name, Nellie McDonnell. Wouldn't it look grand on a book cover? I could be reborn, spotless as the kittens mewing in Molly's closet, erased at last.

Choose me, I countered, offering the kids meat loaf and consistency, promising to be better. They were waiting for their father to demand their loyalty, demanding that they choose him at last, but he stayed mostly away, making short, nervous visits. I became theirs by default, not so much chosen as put up with.

Choose me said the lover, his voice barely audible over the children and parents and animals lined up to present their bills of complaint.

I chose inevitably, passionately, the children, and promised to try to be better for their sake, and they—provisionally, warily—chose me, even knowing that even the meat loaf I promised wouldn't last. I sound cold here, frozen in the formula I was inventing—the *choose me* game—but I was burning with remorse, guilt and yearning.

Every morning I woke, slightly hung over, and squinted up at the plaster dust falling lazily through the air. I could hear the soft whir of Mike's drill and the the tap, tap, tap of his hammer. Every morning I would drag myself out from under the covers, brand new to signify my divorced state. Free at last from the sheets wound round me, I would kick Rox out of bed, push myself through the hall and up the stairs, trip over the cats, and begin pulling my daughter out from under her own lair of comforters and pillows. I would look at her lying there, her long blonde hair falling across her skin, so smooth and so perfect. *Nobody has ever been as pretty as Molly*, I would think. And I wondered what on earth we were doing to each other.

When we had Kitty spayed, Patrick spent an entire afternoon at Coolidge Corner convincing the right candidates to adopt four of her prettiest kittens. He could sell the Brooklyn Bridge, he assured me, sounding jaunty, but in truth he was heartbroken.

So was Roxie. We kept Mouse and Pandora for ourselves, but they were not enough for Roxie's great heart. She spent two days stretched out across the back porch waiting for her missing kittens to bound back up the stairs.

When Kitty came home from the vet's, newly spayed and child-less, the dog sniffed cautiously all over her body, seeming to sense in her a terrible change. Then Rox returned to her mournful vigil at the top of the stairs, waiting patiently for the kittens. She waited for two more days and nights. Finally, after a cold, rainy night, she returned inside to find Mouse and Pandora. And for the first time in months, Kitty was waiting for her, ready to resume their boxing matches on the dining room chair.

The summer of 1988, I began falling in love with David. I don't think I knew that yet. And if I did, I certainly couldn't admit it. "Oh Maa," Molly would have said, "Andrew's father, you're so gross." Five months later, that's exactly what she did say, adding, "Oh yuk."

That's why I repressed the feeling, whatever it was, whenever it bubbled up. I ignored my spells of languor and my sleepless nights. I admitted nothing, except that I was awfully attached to his arms—his arms in the abstract. He'd taken me canoeing, and I sat in the back of the boat, the stern, the stern, not the back, watching him take strong decisive strokes, watching him delicately feather the paddle through the water. His arms, I thought, were lovely, pale as marble; he hardly ever tans, muscled ever so subtly, graceful. I thought about his arms.

I decided that one day I would take Roxie on a canoe trip. First I'd walk her out the front door and take her around the back lot where the car was parked. (Thus we would avoid the dreaded back stairs.) Roxie would sit in the front seat next to me, her head sticking out the window. She would smile and pant and drool all over the car door. She would watch the scenery with great interest and bark in astonishment at the anomalous plaster cows grazing in front of the Hilltop Steak House in Saugus. We would drive by the Leaning Tower of Pizza and the Ship Restaurant and the Half Dollar Bar sign in Danvers, all bark-worthy, and we would continue up Route 1, passing the Topsfield fair grounds, and turn right at an Exxon Station. Two miles down the road we would get to Foote's Canoe Rental.

I would not rent life preservers. Roxie would only chew them up. But I would rent one Grumman 16 foot canoe complete with paddles. The van would drive Roxie and me upstream and leave us to paddle down to the landing. That was the tricky part. I didn't know how to steer a canoe, but I would to ask David to teach me. (I embarrass myself even now thinking of that ploy, even in a fantasy. I never have learned to take the canoe out alone, not once in twenty-five years.)

In my fantasy Roxie sits in the middle of the canoe where she can stare very hard at the shore. Occasionally she barks with approval at the birds flying overhead, the snowy white egret, the fat black crows, and the red winged blackbird. I would like to stop at an island, but there aren't any on this stretch of the Ipswich River.

But this is my fantasy and there will be, after all, one small island where I will land and let Roxie run free. No leash. She dashes back and forth from the shore to the middle, chasing the birds into the air. We swim around the island searching for river clams. Roxie paddles effortlessly next to me, outstripping me, for I am not a strong swimmer, and I watch her head bob next to mine in the dark, tannin-colored water.

After we dry off, I make a fire (with one match) roast a chicken on a spit and bury corn and potatoes in the coals. Roxie and I eat the chicken together and I drink cold white wine.

After a walk down to the water and back again, we sleep under the stars. There's a full moon that night, and soft swirling clouds and there are no mosquitoes. The next morning, we return reluctantly to the canoe to paddle back to Foote's landing. The water is smooth and glassy, reflecting back to us the dark, lush green stand of trees lining the bank.

If only there had been such an island in the Ipswich River. If only I had mastered the J stroke.

How Much is That Doggie in the Window?

I NEVER DID GET ROXIE TO THE ISLAND and she never came close to entering a canoe voluntarily.

A few years later, David and I rented a cottage on Hoel Pond in New Hampshire. We walked her down to the dock with great expectations. But as soon as she saw the canoe bobbing on the water, Roxie stiffened her back, dug her toes into the pier. Uncharacteristically, she bared her teeth and growled, refusing to set one foot into the canoe. We failed many times to coax her in.

Once in desperation we picked her up, David and I, and gently tossed her down into the boat. It was terrible to watch her thrashing around then, trying to keep her balance. She rocked violently back and forth, threatening to turn the boat over until we finally gave up.

And Roxie never entered a boat again. She would only agree to stand up to her knees (illegally) in the Jamaica Pond or to lie on the pier in New Hampshire staring down at the pond. Our Zen dog seemed mesmerized by the sun playing on the water. But no canoe would ever take her to any island. She was too grounded for that.

Stubbornly, sweetly, she defined the terms of her life. In spite of the inbreeding that produced her deafness and her vertigo, she was still, by temperament, a Pedigreed Daughter of Champions. You could never forget that she was fundamentally a show dog bred to strut her stuff at Madison Square Garden. Roxie demanded to be admired all the more as she aged, our canine Gloria Swanson.

"We had faces then," I imagined her saying, as she stalked walkers making their way through the Arboretum.

"That dog, that dog is staring at me," a startled visitor would mutter.

Roxie would be sitting before the speaker, waiting for recognition and praise. Her audience could be understandably confused by such determined and friendly aggression. Embarrassed (for I never became accustomed to her determined stalking), I would suggest just staring back at her with, of course, admiration.

"She's deaf," I'd explain, "and she loves to be seen. She's a show dog."

Roxie would move at this point into a routine that involved much posturing: the wagging of her voluptuous tail, the swishing of her firm and muscular rump and a toss of the head that was positively seductive.

Roxie also spent much time staring out of our front window onto Medfield Street. She balanced herself on her back feet, rested her front legs on the windowsill, and gazed at anybody passing by. I would meet people on the street who asked me about my dog in the window. Roxie had managed to command their attention so thoroughly that whenever she escaped from the condo and ended up on Beacon Street, stopping traffic, her admirers would bring her back to Medfield Street where she belonged.

"I know she lives here," one young woman explained, "because I see her looking out the window. She's become a kind of friend."

Roxie made many breaks for freedom. I don't think she was running away from home. She seemed instead to be looking for a larger audience to appreciate her charms. Sometimes she would head down to the Muddy River where she would be discovered prancing and cavorting and flirting with strollers. Sometimes she danced; teen aged boys especially were quite fascinated by her sense of rhythm. But most often, she headed for Beacon Street and Saint Mary's, across the street from Chef Chang's.

While Roxie was making her mad dashes for freedom, I was getting ready to live with David. In 1989, we decided to buy a house together and spent many weeks looking at houses in Jamaica Plain big enough for all of our kids together. We had four in all, two boys and two girls. Or should I say two young men and two young women—two nineteen year olds and two seventeen year olds. Patrick and Molly and Emily and Andrew formed an ironic post-modern Brady Bunch, one that revealed the dysfunction hidden in the sitcom.

We needed a big house because we wanted to give them all a place to stay whenever they were home from school. Of course we were kidding ourselves. At that time, each kid wanted a private piece of one parent, no sharing, no way. Nothing would have suited them better than a tiny condo with barely room for the two of us, a doll house big enough for only one guest room with one individual name, Patrick or Emily or Andrew or Molly, carved in big letters on the door, which would lock. None of this blended bullshit.

Our blissful ignorance gave us enough energy to hunt for the perfect old house, with room to spare, but we kept losing out in the hot and volatile real estate market. We didn't have enough money, and we didn't have enough faith to enter a market where people were flipping houses like flapjacks.

We decided instead that David could move out of his condo and move into mine. Just for a while, until the market cooled down. But before he did that, we faced an even thornier problem, one that never was properly solved. We needed to do something about the cats. After we spayed Kitty's two daughters, Mouse and Pandora, in the spring of 1989, they changed drastically, missing perhaps their four other brothers and sisters or perhaps missing pieces of themselves.

Pandora ran away quite wildly the second day after her operation. She leapt up into the air, screeched, ran down the porch steps and pressed her body under the fence, never to return. By now Kitty, spayed three months earlier, had become very fat, and spent most of her time curled into a ginger colored ball in the large green bowl on the dining room hutch.

Mouse wandered aimlessly around the house, confusing Roxie by alternating bouts of friendliness with hostile attacks.

Roxie was particularly perplexed by Kitty's lethargic, antisocial state. She would thrust her nose into Kitty's back, waiting for a boxing match, and get instead an irritated hiss and a swipe of bared claws. The only peaceful time for the animals was at night when Roxie and the cats still slept on my bed.

Before David moved in, we needed to find somebody to take the cats, somebody good and loyal and true. This was because Emily was highly allergic to cats and wouldn't be able to visit, let alone stay with us, as long as they were present. Even if we got a bigger place, one that would be large enough to hold all four of the kids, her allergy would keep her away.

That would never work. In fact, it would be terrible. Emily was the lynch pin, a peacemaker necessary to us all. We needed her sweetness and her common sense to make the household work.

But you can imagine the anger, Molly's, and the guilt, mine. Killing the cats, Molly knew, would be just the sort of thing she'd come to expect of me. When I told her that I would find a way to save them, she laughed.

"Nobody will take those cats," she said. "We're their only hope."

Bitterly, she asked why, oh why couldn't I be a normal mother? You know, the kind who didn't get divorced. Just for once couldn't I be the sort of mother who didn't have a lover in the condo taking up her space and making me kill the cats? Just once couldn't I be normal?

"It's David or the cats," I pleaded, "which would you choose?"

"Whatever," she answered. "You always do this."

I called everybody I had ever known trying to give Kitty and Mouse away. I lied, praising their virtues, when in truth they were turning more inward and spooked as we contemplated their fates. I begged Bonnie, a most faithful cat lover, to visit, hoping that she would take them home with her. But we couldn't get Mouse out of the downstairs closet and Kitty refused to leave her bowl. She understandably left without them.

Trying the patience of every animal rescue league from Rhode Island to Maine, we finally ended up at the local MSPCA carrying Kitty and Mouse in their crate. The receptionist smiled cordially, but then she warned us that chances of adoption were extremely slim.

Molly broke in. "We know. You gas them. We know that. You can keep the crate."

I filled out the form relinquishing Kitty and Mouse. Kitty licked my hand and began to purr. It was unbearable. I felt worse about the cats than I had felt about anything I had ever done. It was my fault; everything was my fault, and I would never live this down. And I never have.

Molly ran out of the office. When I reached the car, she was leaning against the door, smoking a cigarette. I knew that she'd been smoking secretly since she was fifteen and she knew that I knew even though I didn't want her to. But this was no time to pick a fight.

"Look," she said, stubbing out the cigarette. (She smoked Kools.) "I want you to be happy, and if David is what it takes, that's okay. But I'll never, never forget the cats, and you can't ever forget them either."

We drove home, and I ordered pizza for dinner. We didn't talk.

Molly and I saw the cats for months afterwards, dashing around the condo. They would spring out of the corners, howl in the darkness, and pounce on our beds. Kitty still rolled into her bowl, while Mouse skidded over the slippery wood floors. And I truly believe that Roxie saw them too. She would whine, run over to me, and tug me by the arm. We were haunted.

With a certain degree of reluctance, David finally moved into the condo with Molly and Roxie and me. His boxes, piled high, took up way too much space, blocking windows and book cases. Roxie kept trying to gnaw on his slippers. Molly shut her door. But she didn't slam it.

She didn't slam it because David possesses a certain degree of calm. Maybe it's his Canadian veneer, for I know now that deep down he's jumping around like a hop toad on a burning pavement. But when the calm kicks in, it can produce a sense of security oddly gratifying to people like Molly and me who've been raised on a steady diet of drama.

David likes games instead of drama. Besides his many boxes and pieces of furniture, he carried into the condo one cribbage board, many decks of cards, and a steady and unquenchable interest in the comics. He read them every morning at breakfast. I was used to reading the *New York Times* with my Granola, regularly getting myself into a twist over the Ayatollah Khomeni and Tiananmen Square and George W.Bush. I never stopped gnashing my teeth over the Exxon Valdez Oil spill, but I did learn that time spent spent with Doonesbury, Dilbert and Zippy could take some of the edge off. Calm can be good.

But David could also, calmly, unwittingly, disrupt the household. I'm not trying to say that he caused Roxie's epilepsy, but he certainly did coincidentally trigger its first manifestation. The night that he moved in, we moved Roxie out of my bed. That was hard to do. I have to admit that I have never known a better bed partner than Roxie. Even the best of men, like David, snore and thrash around. In fact, David seems to play out old Rugby games in his sleep and gives forth quite vividly, with full conviction, physical renderings of play. His arm can shoot out with bedeviled force. I have learned how to catch him before he erupts. As soon as he starts humming and bouncing, I pound him on the back and tell him gently to roll over.

But Roxie, oh Roxie, never erupted. She would lie still and warm and sinuous, stretched out, breathing sweetly, her body curled into mine.

She would lie still until she found herself suddenly exiled. That's when she stretched her great body against the bedroom door and howled. We resisted her lamentations for a half hour. Beaten down, we finally opened the door, and tried to rearrange our bodies with hers, just for one night we told each other. But it was impossible. No careful curling into each other. It just created chaos. Roxie could not stop moving between us and seemed to be determined to push either David or me out onto the floor.

At two in the morning, I finally led her upstairs into the kitchen and locked the childproof gate between her and the dining room. She was used to this spot. I locked her there whenever I left for school. That way I could keep her from eating rugs and glasses and Molly's retainers and my books.

But this time was different. This time, the familiar kitchen lockup threw her into a frenzy. The next morning, I walked upstairs to find Roxie splayed across the floor in a soggy, boneless state, covered in excrement. Her body was twitching very slightly but insistently. I tried to pick her up, but she only sagged back down into a pool of dense flesh. She appeared to be both out of body and out of mind. She didn't know me and she didn't know Molly.

It was David's first day at a new law firm. He was wearing a new blue pinstriped suit and his hair had been razor cut the day before. "Go on," I said, almost meaning it. "Go to work; don't even get near Rox. Not today. You've got to look good."

He turned back to apologize before running down the stairs to his car. "It's probably my fault," he yelled. "I did kick her out of bed."

And then he fled, leaving Molly and me to clean up Rox and get her to the vet.

It was almost impossible to move her. She seemed to be missing her bones and her muscles. Only her twitching suggested that she was capable of movement. We washed and dried her carefully with towels, wrapping her finally in an old bed sheet and wrestled her into the car, for she was roused now into a confused state of animation. After she'd spent twenty-four hours at the vet's, we learned that she was epileptic.

"It's your call," Dr. Groper said. "She's deaf, she's epileptic, and she can't see very well, but God, she's a sweet and beautiful dog." It was not the last time that we would consult Dr. Groper about Roxie's epilepsy. It always helped to know how much he valued her sweetness and her beauty. He was always right about her. She was full of problems, but God, what a sweet and beautiful dog she could be.

Roxie had many other epileptic attacks, but none as dramatic as her first. They all took place in our house in Jamaica Plain. A big house, just like we always wanted—the perfect place for a dog to run off her epileptic attacks or to let them rip.

I do remember a particularly dramatic one on Christmas Eve, minutes before we were sitting down to supper. David, Molly and I took Rox to the vet's, leaving Patrick behind to eat most of the macaroni and cheese.

"I couldn't help it," he said. "I was too worried. I needed comfort food." I made another batch of mac and cheese and we all found comfort.

We needed comfort then. The epilepsy attacks cut to the core of our edgy sense of stability. What did it mean when placid, easy Rox suddenly threw herself down onto the floor to thrash and roll around, banging herself against the wall and the table? What was she telling us when she crashed into our own bodies, almost knocking us over in her seizures? Had we driven her crazy with our enormous needs, our undiminished desires? Or was she just hard wired? For that matter, were we also hard-wired, determined from birth to act out our overwrought genetic histories?

Christmas was hard on all of us that first year that we moved into our house on Prince Street. The season of light and joy provoked great interfamilial wars over the lights themselves, white or colored, and over the crèche, austere or lurid. The ornaments moved family members to tears as they fought over which star ruled. Or would an angel top the tree? If so, which one?

David tried to solve that dispute by buying a third ornament for the top of the tree, only to find it rejected by members of both families. And what sort of tree would it be anyway? No innocent question. Would we pick a Scotch pine from Cambridge or Douglas fir from Concord? David and Patrick kept making emergency runs to Tower records to buy yet another CD—Bing, Frank, Elvis, Fred Waring, Boston Baroque, we've got them all, reminding us how hard it was to satisfy everyone.

If Christmas could produce such tearful discontent, why wouldn't the family stress drive a dog mad? Roxie's epilepsy was probably our fault. Such thoughts didn't resolve themselves, but lay buried, waiting for the next display of a moaning Rox thumping the wainscoting with her hard frenzied head.

We would revise our diagnosis, however, when we would watch Roxie stare with ecstasy at the Christmas candles burning bright. And as our familial differences became familiar, we grew more comfortable with them. We decorated our mantle with dueling mangers.

David's was austere, never allowing more than the simple requisite figures of Mary and Joseph, one shepherd with sheep and the baby Jesus. He faithfully moved the magi around the room all twelve days of Christmas until they were allowed to reach the manger on Twelfth Night.

My manger was full to bursting with Star Wars figures and folk-loric characters and far too many pigs. More like a Bollywood production than something sanctioned by Fred Waring.

We realized over the years that Roxie was as likely to experience an epileptic attack out of the blue on a sunny morning full of birds singing and squirrels chattering as she was in the middle of the night. You could never exactly predict one, but after three or four times, I realized that I was becoming sensitive to a certain tension that Rox would exhibit before she collapsed. I began to notice how she would wake up suddenly out of a sleep, shake herself, stare, and begin to circle the room nervously, looking for a way to escape. I learned how to let her out into the garden where she would run around in careful circles tracing and retracing the round brick walk enclosing the day lilies. She looked like a racehorse trotting around the track, able, through those crazy periods of unexpected exercise, to run off her malady.

One April morning, as I sat reading Trollope on the living room sofa, Roxie started shaking. I could feel her moving against me, trying to push herself onto my lap. As soon as she began to twitch, I got down on the floor and covered her body with mine. I gently massaged her head.

We lay there together for almost an hour. I could feel her spasms move out of her into me, but somehow my own body contained them, and they went no farther. We were locked together in a strange rhythm that I was somehow controlling or at least keeping safe. The spasms relaxed me; I almost fell asleep, rocked by her body—safe, somehow while I was keeping her from erupting. And suddenly it was over. Roxie stopped shaking, and began gently snoring.

When I finally lifted myself off, she turned her head up towards me with a certain degree of irritation, as if to say, what on earth are you doing down here? I went back to my Trollope, while Roxie slept, stretched out in the sunlight.

If only I could have done that to the kids, just dropped down on the floor to lie next to them, making them still and safe without squashing them. But they were not so easily pacified. So often we disappointed them, unexpectedly, as if by magic. What buttons did we push? What powers did we still unwittingly possess?

When we found our house on Prince Street in Jamaica Plain in 1990, Arts and Crafts, with a tiny yard in back, it needed two months of renovation.

I decided that Roxie had to be introduced to her new home gradually. Would I ever stop projecting my desires and needs onto a dumb, deaf animal? Because of course I was the one who needed the visits, all those visits to watch the builders put up the deck and install the new kitchen designed to look as if it had always been there since 1911.

I merely imagined Roxie's fascination with the scraping and banging and plastering. When she tugged on the leash, I decided that she wanted to see more, not less, and eagerly pulled her up to the third floor. Always obliging, she sniffed the corners and stared out the windows, looking perhaps for Kitty, or at least for an escape route.

Three days before our move, the builders were still frantically sanding and polyurethaning the floors. David and I could smell the fumes as we stood with Don, our contractor, in the basement. While we admired the freshly sanded kitchen cabinets, tongue and groove, designed to match the wainscoting, Roxie suddenly disappeared. She must have wandered up the basement stairs into the body of the house. No wonder. Bunkered all the way down in the basement, we were getting sick from the smell. How much more powerful it must have been for her sensitive nose. Agony. Or was she seeking it out drunkenly, breathing it in with great pleasure?

Whatever the reason, she was gone. David took off his shoes to save the floors and took after her. Don and I stayed downstairs, worried about the state of the polyurethane. We could only imagine the mess that Roxie was making. But suddenly we heard a scrambling, and then a thumping.

David yelled down to us, "Get outside, Rox is in the street. She's jumped out the window."

We ran out the basement bulkhead, down the driveway, into the street, but it was empty.

It was a Tuesday morning, and the neighbors were all at work. I ran up and down wildly, waving my arms, doing semaphore, how else to communicate with a deaf dog? And there she was, five houses down, across the street, standing on somebody's doorstep. She stood squarely on her four feet, shuddering, shaking her head wildly. Blood splashed from her nose onto my pants, my shoes, and onto the neighbor's door.

Months later, we met our neighbors for the first time. They had always wondered why their porch had been so mysteriously splattered in blood.

I threw my sweater over Roxie to stop her shaking. She looked up at me, her eyes rolling back into their sockets, locked into a state of confusion impossible to penetrate.

"It'll be all right, Rox, you're in one piece," I murmured, knowing that she couldn't hear me.

David ran over, still in his stocking feet. He had gone, he said, through every room in the house and, on his way up the stairs to the third floor, he heard a scuttling noise. The low bedroom window was open. David rushed over to see Roxie standing stunned in the middle of the street. He had just missed her flight.

What is most remarkable is that nobody on Prince Street had seen her fly. Roxie, a minor daughter of Daedalus, plunged down onto the porch roof and rolled off onto the lawn before staggering onto an indifferent pavement. No witnesses. Just a trail of blood that had gushed from her nose.

We wrapped her in David's jacket and drove to Angell Memorial, the MSPCA hospital nearby, where we were immediately suspected of committing crimes against the animal world.

"Dogs don't jump out of windows," the intern on call told us; "cats might, but not dogs."

"She was raised by cats," I feebly explained, but I could see by the steely look in her eye that she had already decided that we had abused Roxie, given her a bloody nose and were trying to excuse our crimes by concocting an unlikely story about freedom and flight. Roxie didn't much like the interrogation, and started to bristle and even growl.

The intern offered us two options. We could take Roxie home and wait and see, or we could leave her at the hospital where they would sedate her and examine her for internal injuries. Roxie kept growling and started to attack the floor with her nails.

We drove her back to the condo, watching over her with curious and confused interest. *Wait and see what*, I wondered, but after a day or two she seemed herself once more.

Well, not exactly herself. We could barely get her out of the door for a walk, and when we did move into our new house, it took us two weeks to get her to walk out of the French door into the garden. Doors, particularly doors with windows, had become her enemies, leading her into free fall that ended in bloody disaster.

In the Prince Street house, Roxie became our homey, dedicated to keeping the domestic flame burning. When I wasn't at school, I worked on the sofa, where I either read or wrote. Rox was either curled up beside me, or sprawled across the Turkish rug, looking like a dog in an advertisement for whiskey or expensive perfume.

She reeked of privilege, our Akita, light and dense, marking her place before the hearth. She would only stir if I moved out of the room and, then, deaf and arthritic, she would shake herself into consciousness, and primly follow me to my fairly banal destination. The bathroom, the kitchen, the study, the backyard, all of these places she would visit with me, patiently, obligingly, until once more she was released to flop down onto the rug, as far away from the windows as she could get.

DIXIE ON MY MIND

THE HOUSE DID ALL THAT A HOUSE COULD DO. We bought two beds for the third floor, one for Molly, who got the biggest room with more light because she sometimes lived with us, and one for Emily, who got the smaller, but snugger and sweeter room. We bought two futons for the second floor, one for Andrew, one for Patrick; they were in David's study and the TV room, and pretty much up for grabs. First come first served for boys soon to be men.

After she graduated from Tufts, Molly ended up living in various other places, always in Boston, always with roommates, and didn't really need her room any longer. So her room, known forever after as Molly's room, became anybody's in need of one. Beds filled and emptied while closets burst with the boxes and hangers and books and baseball cards of four lives. The overflow ran down the stairs and into the basement where identical collections of Roald Dahl and Richard Scarry and Star Wars figures took on the distinct odor of beloved neglect.

Our so-called "blending" sometimes curdled. Patrick and Andrew specialized in theatrical displays that displaced real emotion. Patrick excelled in cheesy comedy, producing a college television program called The Velveeta's. He also interned in horror movies, and got to meet the guy who directed *Night of the Living Dead*.

Andrew was becoming a genuine actor, taking professional dramatic roles in Shakespearian and sit-com productions from Nova Scotia to Vancouver. The girls were less comical, more earnest. It could be that Molly and Emily took family more seriously than their brothers did. Perhaps black humor was no more satisfying than the disappointment that inspired it. For we did, too often, disappoint them.

The house did what it could, while we worked on keeping the household gods straight. We became the family archivists, packing up memories to store in the attic and basement. That is why, one Thanksgiving weekend in the mid nineties, David and I drove up to Newburyport to pick up boxes – yes, more boxes, that I had stored in Denny's attic.

After the divorce, while the condo was being turned into a construction site, there had been no room to store the doll house, the train set, the soccer game, two cartons of books like *Ant and Bee, Frog and Toad, In the Night Kitchen, Katy and the Big Snow*, three cases of Cynar—don't even ask—and a punch bowl with eighteen glasses never used even once. These treasures now resided in the Jefferson Street attic in Newburyport, the last dusty remains of my first marriage.

"You've got to pick them up," Denny wrote, "the house is almost sold."

He'd stopped talking to me in May 1994, the day after Molly graduated from college, his fiscal and emotional obligations ended. *Finito*, he wrote.

His decided acts of separation always threw me off balance. Why should it matter that he refused to talk to me any more, that he spoke to the kids once a year at most? Why should I be so angry? Why did I feel abandoned?

Denny, his wife Lois and their daughter, Chiara, had moved to California. Berkeley, California is where we had lived as a family— without animals—from 1968 to 1975.

California was my place. Of course, such territorial fantasies shocked me. Why shouldn't Denny wish to move back to a place of such sensuous and voluptuous pleasure, where the hills thrust up maternally, and the sun drops into the bay, turning it the color of molten gold? I really was a selfish person after all, only pretending not to hold grudges tightly to my wounded breast. I wanted everything to belong to me always.

So there we were, on a dank and dreary November afternoon (in Berkeley the sun would be breaking through the fog), David and I, reluctantly calling on Lois's mother, who had been watching Dixie and the house.

Denny said Lois's mother needed to be in the house—"on the premises"—for insurance reasons until the house was sold, but his reasoning seemed odd to me. I did know that Denny was asking too much for the place in a bad housing slump and that, actually, nothing was moving, no matter how low the price. But I still couldn't understand what Dixie was doing in Newburyport. Why wasn't she in California playing Happy Families?

Because, Denny told the kids before he left Boston, because *you could not rent* in California if you had a dog. Period. They were going out "to explore their options." You could see how Dixie would make that difficult, he said.

They would send for her when they owned their own place. It was simple, he told the kids. *No problemo.* I knew that when he talked like that, the conversation would end, *Rapidito.* And I figured that deep down he was lying. Like his kids, Dixie would soon be *Finito.*

Lois's mother and Roxie's mother were living together—quite happily, it turned out—in the tiny house that Denny and I had bought on the river in our last-ditch efforts to save the dying, dried out body of our marriage in 1985, or was it 1986? Whenever, it was too late.

Denny had spent three months driving in a circle drawn around Boston, looking at weekend places that were between one and two hours away. He argued that the Newburyport house would reproduce, or even improve upon, the Pocono country house. But I didn't want to start over, working hard again on a country house.

By then I was teaching at Tufts, no longer commuting between NYU and Brookline. I dreamed of staying in one place, not girding up to find, buy, furnish, landscape, clean, and perhaps ruin another place. The redemptive potential of a new space seemed an illusion, I said, it was doomed to fail.

But Denny had always been able to tune out my warnings, so it was no surprise to find ourselves driving up to Newburyport, a sweet and good place, relatively unspoiled, on the Merrimack River, ten minutes from Plum Island. It was perfect—except for us.

We bought the house in the dark. After five hours of driving around town, I finally got my hands on the real estate bible that the real estate agent kept in her glove compartment. She was drifting into sleep and Denny, still droning on, was starting to get difficult. But once I got hold of the book, my talent for research kicked in.

I even got kind of excited when I found the small, lovely house near the river. It had been built before the Civil War in a style too modest to be given a name. It was a tiny house, a child's idea of a house. Straight lines intersected into a high-pitched slate roof. How I loved that roof. Even when Denny painted the white house a lurid shade of blue after the divorce (yes, I am a territorial bitch), the slates remained, gleaming, full of a calm, almost indifferent, integrity.

I have always liked the way houses look at night. These windows shone sharp and clear in the darkness, like lights and candles welcoming us in. Inside was less promising. An oversized stone fireplace dominated the spare angular space. A steep simple staircase shot straight up into the small, spare rooms on the second floor that looked out onto the river.

We couldn't see the river that night, but we knew from the map that it rushed by, full then of ice floes, full later of bird song that drew visitors by the carload to the end of our street. They would run down Jefferson Street to the landing armed with binoculars and cameras, stalking the elusive eagles living on the island that was so close we could almost touch it. But we didn't see the river that night; we only saw the idea of a house that might promise relief from ourselves.

We didn't deserve the place. We never spent the time or energy it would take to restore the house to its original modest intentions. We huddled instead on weekends before the preposterous fireplace. I concocted healthy alcoholic drinks, vodka and anything in the vegetable or fruit family that I could fit into the juicer, while Denny watched anything on cable television. Mostly the kids stayed back in Brookline with friends, probably bad for their moral development but sensible nonetheless. They were right to stay out of our way.

146

One exceptional night, Patrick and his Dungeon and Dragon friends drove up with me to play "Call of Cathulu," in honor of H.P. Lovecraft. I chaperoned the boys while they searched for scary clues, pails full of kidneys, buried bones, fragments of maniacal diaries forged by Patrick, the master sleuth.

But most of the times, Denny and I didn't even stay the night, worried about the teenage angst erupting in our absence. Dixie of course was always with us.

I walked Dix all over Newburyport. It really is a lovely town, and it was even better in the late eighties, before so many of the sweet little houses were stretched into McMansions. We would get to the harbor, and I'd look out onto the water wondering what on earth we were doing. Dixie would look up at me anxiously. She had become more connected to me. I wouldn't have wanted to be my dog on those late weekend afternoons, but that was her job —taking care of me.

It was hard to return to Newburyport to get my boxes out of the attic. I was nervous about being with Dixie. I had only seen her once after the divorce and it had been a disaster.

It was during the winter of 1987. Roxie, her daughter, must have been at least four months old then. Denny walked into the condo, pulling Dix on the leash, and I could see at once that she had been shockingly transformed. She was no longer the strong, sensual creature who had exerted so much power over us. Even her coloring had changed. She seemed bleached out, vacant, not her fawn-and-brown colored, mean and ornery self. Not loving, not aggressively affectionate, not anything at all that I could recognize.

I looked for the real Dixie, tough and tantalizing and found, instead, a dog that just stood there looking at us blankly, registering nothing. Nothing, that is, until she saw her daughter Roxie. Suddenly, with frantic energy, she strained at the leash. Denny, surprised, let her free. She ran after Rox, teeth bared, making a dangerous guttural sound. Perhaps remembering the way Dixie had mistreated her in the kennel, Roxie ran behind the sofa. Dixie kept throwing herself at the wall next to the sofa, too big to get into her daughter's hideaway. She looked ghostly, dead white, and so thin you could almost see through her. *What did they do to her in the kennel*, I wondered? How had they produced this spectral, maniacal dog bent on attacking poor Rox? Her daughter stayed put, not even whimpering.

Denny asked me then and there, raising his voice to be heard over Dixie's bark, if I would please take Dixie off his hands.

"You see," he said in a strained, high-pitched way, "Dix doesn't seem too happy in Newburyport, missing the kids and all. Wouldn't it be good to have her and her puppy? Wouldn't the kids like to have her back? Wouldn't it make little Roxie happy?"

Little Roxie stayed still and silent behind the couch.

I wanted to scream at him. How could Dixie stay here? Why can't you see how hard it would be to take her? Why couldn't you ever see how hard things could get?

Instead I apologized. "I'm sorry, I'm really sorry," I said, "but I can't. Look at them now."

I gestured at Dixie. She was growling. "We live in such a small space. We don't have room for their fighting, for all this agony. How can you ask me to do this?"

Molly cut in, angrily. "Get real," she said; "Dixie would chow down Rox in a minute."

Denny and Dixie quickly left together. *What if I had said yes*, I wondered? Could I have made Dixie sign a peace treaty with her daughter?

I looked out the window and watched Dixie walk to the car with Denny, and I imagined, just for the moment, my old fantasy of happy families. In it I am a good parent, the best parent, the one with the beautifully behaved Akitas, mother and daughter strutting their stuff.

Now that the old Dixie had been erased, I wrote over her blankness and turned her into a loving mother, a model citizen happy to walk up and down the Riverway off leash, under command. The kids would flourish, their confidence in me restored, their faith in themselves growing. We would be whole, the kids, the dogs and me.

Why did I think I could ever be capable of imprinting my domestic fantasies onto my animals? Maybe somebody else, that philosopher from Yale who trains pit bulls, maybe she was up to the challenge, but I stood still, watching Denny and Dixie from the window until his car drove down Medfield Street and out of sight.

Poor Rox, hiding from her cruel mother, didn't come out from behind the sofa for hours, not until she needed to pee. I called my mother then, my ear half off the receiver as she barked and growled at me. I was making amends to Rox.

David and I parked on Jefferson Street, two doors up from the house, because I wanted to show him the river running by and the bird pre-serve on the island across from the end of the street. We stood on the bank, looking over the dark water. The sun was in the process of set-ting, but there would be no transcendental production tonight; it was cold, gray, hardscrabble here on a bank that I had always loved to stand on.

"This is," I insisted, too softly to be understood, "a beautiful spot, just not now. But you should have seen it when…."

I stopped mumbling, aware that I was trying to prove too much. Why did we need a sunset? What did the house mean anyway? A discarded terrain scarred with old memories best forgotten, but here it loomed up, full of one more pile of boxes, reminders of what we couldn't keep but couldn't exactly throw away.

We walked back to the house. Dixie, front paws pressed against the window, looked out at me with extraordinary joy. You could feel her tail wagging. As we walked up to the door, we could see her push her head against the glass and bark triumphantly. I am not projecting this enthusiasm onto her. She really remembered me.

On Monmouth Street, Dixie used to lie next to me on the sofa while I stroked her and sang. I sang to her the way I did to the kids, doing sing-and-soft, singing to them all about their exploits, their characters, their sweetness. Naming them by their names. And when I would did that to Dixie, she would sing back, crooning and moan-ing, in a rhythm that we developed together.

Her remoteness when Denny had brought her to the condo had been made even more shocking by my memories of those periods of deep intimacy, an intimacy erased by her bleached and disoriented presence. *Now what*, I wondered? What would I do if I found the old Dix, the loving Dix, bullying, difficult, but connected intimately to me and to the kids?

We rang the bell, and waited. Lois's mother answered; she'd been waiting for us, she told us, and she knew that Dixie had been waiting too. Meanwhile, Dix was prancing around on four feet and then two, jumping up on me, licking me all over, crooning and crying, blowing into me her strong, sweet dog breath. Standing up, she was as tall as me.

When she put her arms around my shoulders, and licked me and began to sing, I couldn't bear it. "God," said David, "I can't believe how much she looks like Rox. Rox with a gray muzzle."

"And not as vain," I said, "not as vain as Rox."

Dixie was never proud of her looks, only her talent for terrorizing.

Lois's mother seemed calm and confident, capable of taking the edge off Dixie. "We're such good friends," she said, "Dixie and I take such wonderful walks around town. Why you should see how everybody loves to see us come down the street. Dixie wags her tail, and sometimes she dances."

Dixie dancing; what on earth? Dixie never danced. I just stared. "Come on, Dixie," she crooned, "give us a little dance." And she did, turning her big body around in circles, wagging her tail, seeming pleased with herself. Dixie dancing like a circus dog.

"Next," I said, "you'll be telling me that she likes to fetch."

Lois's mother laughed. "Oh no, she's much too refined for that. Akitas don't fetch."

We moved into the attic, Dix behind us, sniffing, groaning and not letting us out of her sight. We opened boxes—too painful, those boxes. As much as we had thrown out those days in Brooklyn, we had still managed to save so many things impossible to defend, broken down and chipped remnants barely worth resurrecting. But there was Dixie, licking me, pushing me as we carried the train set and the doll house, the books and the punchbowl out from the attic down into the car. And now she was Dixie, nuzzling, holding onto to me for dear life, insisting that I must not go.

"You be sure to visit us again," Lois's mother said. "Dixie's going to miss you, aren't you girl?"

She bent down to cup Dixie's snout and looked deep into her eyes.

"I think," she said, "I'll give you a little walk right away, that'll cheer you up, won't it, good girl?"

She grabbed the leash from the mantle, and snapped it quickly onto Dixie's collar.

"Good girl," she said, "good girl."

We all left the house together, David and Dixie and Lois's mother and me. Dixie prancing in excitement, ready to charm the neighbors, ready to dance on command. What kind of dog would she have been, I wondered, if she had always lived with Lois's mother? What wonderful tricks could she have performed? How many puppies would she have borne, none of them deaf?

"Bye, Dix," I cried, rubbing her ears that were getting a little bald but were still perky, those iconic signs of her Akita pedigree. Which ear was it that I had massaged so long ago, the one that flopped down so dangerously? The left one? I couldn't remember, but I could still feel it in my hands.

"Bye, good girl, stay good, stay happy," I said. "Good girl."

And we watched her turn to walk slowly down Jefferson Street, being good.

Shortly after that night, the house finally sold. Lois's mother went back to her own life where there was no room for Dixie. Denny told the kids that he sent Dixie to a ranch for dogs in Montana, or maybe it was Wyoming, where dogs ran free all day long and lived idyllic lives of hardy luxury.

Can we visit her, the kids wanted to know?

Denny didn't think so. Later he told them that an energetic and loving couple from Vermont had been driving through Wyoming. They stopped at the ranch and, just like that, they fell love with Dixie. She lives with them now, he told them, on their farm.

Can we see her, they asked him?

Denny didn't think so. "The ranch policy for adoptions prohibits visits from former family members. You know how it is," he said.

"Whatever," Molly said. "Whatever."

"She's dead," Patrick said. "Dead and gone to doggy heaven. No visitors."

I like to imagine Dixie on a farm, hanging out with Wilbur, chasing Henrietta the Rhode Island Red. She could growl at the raccoon marauding the bird feeder. I can almost see her dancing, forgiving me for not saving her.

ROXIE, ROXIE, BURNING BRIGHT

FOR YEARS ROXIE HAD DISLIKED small children, barking fiercely at any kid intrepid enough to approach her. As she aged, she seemed to sweeten and began seeking children out, prancing before them to try out her show-dog tricks. Bony and frail, she still showed off her splendid coat, but she lacked the muscular vitality that show dogs need to attract an audience.

As her knees became knobby and her muzzle gray and stiff, she became pliant and patient, allowing two and three year olds to poke her and pat her. Sometimes she would even lick the face of a particularly insistent admirer. After such a display of her waning powers, she would always look up at me with a measured degree of triumph. I can still, she would suggest, strut my stuff.

Roxie's hunger for admiration really kicked in on holidays. Patrick, Molly, Emily and Andrew would all be together, not for the holiday itself, but for the express purpose of scratching her elbows and rubbing her neck. She'd barely move from her central spot on the rug, accepting her due, waiting for more.

Christmas was the best of those times, when neighbors would drop in, bearing gifts, a bone, and perhaps, a squeeze toy. Maybe it was the lights on the tree, the logs burning in the fireplace, the candles on the mantle, wrapping paper covering the floor, and all those cameras flashing, aimed at her in the center of the room. Maybe it was just the smell of prime rib roasting for hours in the oven. Whatever the reason, Roxie was usually awake for most of Christmas day, getting underfoot.

Every year I bought a plum pudding two months before Christmas to begin drowning it in brandy. After steaming it, I'd warm more brandy, flame it, pour it over the pudding, and carry it into the darkened dining room.

The flame burnt blue, mysteriously, concentrating all of the lights of Christmas day into one small, dramatic space.

One Christmas night, Roxie, old and stubborn, seemed to be more underfoot than usual. I had been bumping into her all day and, as I moved slowly into the dining room, pudding plate in both hands, I tripped over her standing in the doorway. I watched in horror as the flaming brandy cascaded down onto her back. Her hairs stood straight up, turning blue and gold. A line along her back was defined by the flame. She didn't blink and she didn't budge, as the fire danced up and down and around her. She simply gazed ahead at the candles on the table, eyes shining, seemingly pleased that everybody at the table rose up to watch her blaze. Roxie, burning bright, stood still, so serenely magnificent, so sublimely indifferent to the tongues of fire playing on her back.

A minute later, it was all over. The flame burnt out and Roxie, unscathed, not one hair singed, started working on her bone under the table.

As she aged, her mellow forbearance and sublime indifference became downright dangerous. Her deafness had always kept her from being territorial. She was quick to defer to the doggy needs of her peers. Take that bone, she seemed to say; I'd love to share it with you. Have a doggy chew while you're at it.

One Spring day in the Arnold Arboretum, she moved dreamily over to greet an old blind dog tottering unsteadily across the path. His molting coat of dusty black hair turning gray barely covered his scrawny, trembling frame and his sightless eyes looked desperate and wild. The closer Rox came to the dog, the louder the dog growled.

"She doesn't like to be around dogs," her owner said nervously. "She doesn't like what she can't see."

Too late, Rox was already within striking distance. The old dog opened his mouth and bit down hard onto Roxie's nose, drawing blood.

Roxie backed up, shook her head, and looked up at me, wagging her tail. Wagging her tail?

"Was it good for you, Rox?" I asked.

Close encounters in the Arboretum? Rox just shook her head once more, and walked back home with me, humming.

Roxie's beauty could still grab your heart. When David and I decided to get married in May 1997, we had the wedding in our house. To do it right, we had a proper piper, kilt and all, playing in the garden. Roxie's ears stood high, as she sat grinning, seeming to listen to "The Nut Brown Maid."

In most of the wedding pictures Roxie always seems to be sitting square in the middle of the frame, blessing us with a sweetness that was beginning to wear out along with the rest of her.

The walks became shorter and more painful. Senile, arthritic, Rox would drag herself to the end of the block, shake herself and stare up at me in confusion. You could watch her forget where she was, who she was, and why she was finding herself suddenly in the middle of the street. Where was the rug? Once, after only two or three houses, she jumped imperiously into the air and turned her body around to stare up at me with real anger. "Do you want to go back home?" I asked, always forgetting not to talk to her, and we made our way back up the street to our door.

She also became incontinent, a condition that gave her great pain. Rox was such a delicate and scrupulous dog that even in blizzards and hurricanes, she refused to pee in the back yard, an apparently sacred spot that needed to be free of her bodily pollution. The dribbles of pee and the hard pellets of poop seemed to humiliate her. She hid some of the turds, pushing them under the sofa, behind doors, staring up at me with amazement when I uncovered her treasures.

When she turned eleven, I began to wonder about putting her to sleep. I couldn't keep dragging her down the front steps onto the sidewalk. I tried instead to pull her down the back stairs into the garden. The twilight world of smells that she used to love only irritated her. As did my comforting words, truly falling on deaf ears.

But every so often, she would rouse herself, shake her body, and

157

take a notion to drag me along with her down the sidewalk, determined to get somewhere at last. The winter before she died, she became quite unruly on the leash, pulling me into snow banks and knocking me over in icy patches. I had to admit that things were getting out of hand. Certainly she was getting out of my hand. What if she broke away from me and staggered into the street?

I wondered then if dogs got Alzheimer's. I thought about the condition all of the time. My mother in Chicago was also crashing into anything that got in her way. Like Roxie, she stared up at me with wild and terrified eyes, seeing everything and nothing at all. I don't know who worried me more then—my mother, my dog or to be honest, myself. I do know that whenever I watched over my mother, I imagined myself in her place, inheriting her debilitating disease.

In the first years of her Alzheimer's, she raged against her condition, but as it worsened, her anger began to dissolve along with her memory. The last year of her life, 1998, she even seemed to love me, but I didn't know then what to do with the love; it seemed too preposterously unfamiliar.

Who was she seeing when she kissed me so gently? She insisted that I was her long lost girlfriend from her sorority in college. Dolores, that's what she called me. She wanted to trade secrets about our boyfriends. "I'll show you mine," she said, pulling out a picture of her and my dad at somebody's funeral, taken maybe ten or eleven years before. She stared at it hard, trying to hold it in place, reminding me of Roxie then, struggling for focus.

"I don't know her," she said, "but I can tell that she doesn't like him. He likes her, though. Too bad for him," she laughed.

I failed her then, one last time, trying to make her remember who I was. I was wrong. I know that now. I should have played along with her fantasy. She always been so ashamed of not going to college. She quit school at age sixteen to help support her family. I knew that. Why wouldn't she want to make me her sorority sister instead of her daughter?

"But I am not Dolores," I said. I" am not your sorority sister. I am me," I said, thinking at the same time that I was the daughter who

158

always failed her. The one she knew how to hurt. I was myself, I insisted—the one who learned how to hurt back. How had she forgotten? Where did this sloppy warmth come from, this imaginary insistence that she loved me? Loved me, or loved Dolores? I remained cold and numb. The splinter of ice planted in my heart so long ago could not melt away.

The last time I saw my mother, the third week in December, just when Clinton was being dragged through congress for his sins, I returned to Boston for the worst Christmas I've ever ruined. Maybe my mother was haunting me prematurely. I should have let her call me Dolores after all. I remember cleaning potatoes in front of the television, watching the Impeachment hearings. How could everything have gotten so screwed up? I wondered, imagining a future controlled by zealots.

We were all driven by angry spirits that Christmas—David and I, and all of the kids. All of us except Roxie, who still waited to watch the plum pudding burst into flames. We weren't as patient as Rox. Instead we all seemed to spontaneously combust. Burning shards of domesticity flew through the air, almost igniting the tree drying out in the corner. All the old grudges, sharpened, refined, wounded in turn each and every one of us.

At the end of it, David and I couldn't even look at each other. Everything felt dead and not quite buried.

After my mother died in early January 1999, David and I went to a couples' therapist, reeling from the anger we couldn't get rid of, the betrayal we kept trying to master and understand. Barbara our therapist was brilliant, incisive, and fast.

"Why did you get married," she asked? "You were together what —nine years or so?"

"Or so," we admitted.

"Why did you decide just then," she asked, bearing down now. "Why then?"

We stumbled around, trying to explain that we did it for the kids. We thought we'd be a good example. It was embarrassing to deliver such a laughable notion.

"They seemed stuck," we said. "We thought they needed to see us stable, united, you know."

"No, I don't know," she said. "People get married for their own reasons. Marriage is a pretty personal business. You get married for yourself." she said, more softly. "Don't you know that?"

I guess we didn't. She set up another appointment. "There's more to life than caretaking," she said, smiling, as she closed the door.

While we tried to pay attention to our own problems, Roxie kept right on going, filled with her own serene energy. She outlived my mother by six months. Every day seemed likely to be her last, but she refused to die on my watch.

If we hadn't gone to California for Patrick's wedding, she might have lived years more, painful years watching over us, another benighted, confused caretaker, desperate not to fail us.

Animals will do almost anything to stay alive for their owners. Though owner cannot be the right word. By now Roxie owned us completely. We were bound to her, in love and fear. I wanted to release her, but I didn't know how. Not when she would lay her head on my lap, her broad, heavy, noble head still covered in soft hairs that stood up all over, waiting for my touch. I still knew where to rub her—the tender parts under the top of her legs and at the back of her knees. I massaged her feet with oil; the pads had cracked with age. And of course I rubbed her belly, the one part of her body that still seemed supple and full of life.

On June 16, 1999, Patrick and Kari were married in Calistoga, California, in the middle of a vineyard. The sun was blazing down, bleaching out the intense color of the grapes growing in carefully ordered rows. Denny was there, of course, as Patrick's father, still related to Roxie through Dixie, though Dixie was long gone, abandoned, *Finito.*

Denny was creating minor crises. He was supposed to have arrived in Calistoga but was not answering phone calls. He never did show up for the tapas party the night before the wedding ceremony. He'd been feeling poorly, he explained, finally calling in his excuse around midnight just as the party was breaking up. Next morning, at the very last second, he slipped into the chair next to mine in the first row. I could see Patrick's strained, white face begin to relax when he saw his father.

At exactly five o'clock, California time, Patrick and Kari said their vows to a woman named Blue to the tunes of Barry White.

Molly was back in Boston, nursing her newborn daughter, Caitlin, barely two months old. At exactly eight o'clock, Boston time, the same moment that Patrick and Kari were married, Roxie lay down and died in the kennel. She had been for a walk, not a bad walk as things went for her then. Indeed, it sounded as if she had taken a splendid final walk along the Muddy River outside the animal hospital.

I learned about her walk from the Veterinary Attendant who had taken her up and down the stairs, out to the river and back. After the walk, Roxie circled her blanket, shook herself, releasing her soft hairs into the air, flopped down, and stretched out. Ten minutes later, the attendant checked on her and discovered her body. Somewhere in my atheistic soul, I believe that Roxie was able to die just then because her work was finally over—a baby for Molly and a wedding for Patrick. That sweet and hard-working dog of divorce had done her job.

I knew none of this when we returned late in the night to Jamaica Plain. We crawled into bed, planning to pick up Rox the next morning. Molly called us at 6:30 in the morning, breathless.

"Ma, don't go to the vet's to get Rox," she said, and then she started to cry. "She died," she said, "but I didn't want you to find out until you got back."

I visited the animal hospital that afternoon to find out what we needed to do.

"Can I see her?" I asked, "Is it alright if I touch her?" It was her body I craved, the feel of her great bones, her hair, and her sweet solid flesh. I wanted to curl into her. Dr. Groper came out to tell me that I probably wouldn't want to see Rox in her condition.

He winced. "She's frozen, you see, and she's in a kind of ghastly position."

He loved Rox for all of her ailments and for all of her beauty. He thought hard, and then offered to thaw her so that I could see her one more time.

"Oh God no," I said, I couldn't even imagine such a macabre transformation from the ghastly frozen to the practically perfect thawed, but I did admire his ingenuity.

How to memorialize a frozen dog? Burying her in the yard seemed too great an operation to conduct in such a small space, a minor Big Dig. I remembered Sissy's grave. A hole big enough for Sissy used up a lot of vacant land. Our tiny garden was planted over in bamboo and day lilies, oregano and rosemary, red currants, raspberries and primroses, and the beds were lined with brick walks. Where would we find room for Rox? And what would happen after we all moved? I didn't like the idea of Roxie alone underground, moldering.

In Japan, the Akita is a temple dog, a sacred animal. To demonstrate their loyalty to the breed, owners used to hang their dead dog's skin on the wall, in memory of the animal's spirit. When I first learned about this practice, I was horrified, but as I watched Rox become older and stiffer, her mortality prodded me into imagining ways to preserve pieces of her beauty.

The hair of an Akita is indeed worth memorializing. The fur comes in two layers, one layer of under hairs that are strong and silky and another of soft and fuzzy upper hairs that keep shedding all over the house.

Once I met a woman in the Arboretum who asked me for some of Roxie's hair. She was a weaver and wanted to spin the hairs into wool for her loom. I was grooming Roxie when we met. Rox hated being brushed or combed, but seemed to enjoy standing under the trees letting my fingers run through her heavy and often sticky hairs. I used to collect several plastic bags full of the hairs before they could blow into the pussy willows. I handed over the bags of hair gladly. I liked the idea of Roxie being woven into somebody's tapestry. Better than being stuffed—David's ironic solution to the preservation of Roxie's beauty. He imagined her as a doorstop, lacquered and flamboyant, her tail eternally curled.

We cremated Roxie, Roxie burning bright, transforming her tired body into ashes and bright shards of bone. We stored her in an urn that my neighbor Ann, made for her. It looks like a Victorian Ginger

Jar and sits on the mantle. I have scattered her ashes about five differ-ent times, most notably at a large party, involving a march to Jamaica Pond. We stopped at that place on the pond where Roxie spent so much of her time up to her ankles contemplating the sun on the water.

David threw a handful of ashes out into the pond shouting, "Okay, Rox, this is it. At last you're going to get out there past your knees and all the way over your head. You are finally going to get all wet."

And she did.

MY LAST DOG

To understand why David and I became so entangled with Ben, the manic Border Collie, you need to know something about our addiction to discomfort.

That's not exactly accurate. We have a certain talent for making other people comfortable—friends, children, students, clients, our neighbors, and even our enemies. Well, sometimes. Let's say that we try. Think of us as low level comfort facilitators working to make people feel easy. Other people. But we find it difficult to do this for ourselves.

Sometimes we drank too much instead. Drinking can take the edge off caretaking.

In fact our story is an unexceptional one, almost too ordinary, repeated over and over through the seventies and eighties and nineties. Only the animals are extraordinary. We began our lives in the Midwest, David in Northern Ontario, me in Chicago, and we became academics who specialized in Eighteenth Century English Literature, married other people, had kids, two each, one boy, one girl, same ages, and finally met in Boston in 1985.

The meeting itself was not dramatic, but if you mapped our meeting it would look as if it had been ordained. There would be David coming from Thunder Bay to Toronto to London to Rochester to Buffalo and finally to Boston. I would be coming from Chicago and Oxford, Ohio to Champaign-Urbana to Providence, Rhode Island to Boston to Berkeley to London to New York (see chapter on pigs) to Boston.

And there we met, eating Bratwurst at Schroeder's German Restaurant, talking about our children (Molly and Andrew actually knew each other) and of course about eighteenth-century writers like Johnson and Boswell and Fielding.

We stayed in touch. I invited him to my annual New Years Day Party and he gave me the name of my wonderful divorce lawyer. And then, in 1988, we truly came together. All of us: Patrick and Emily and Molly and Andrew and, of course, Roxie.

They called it "blending" then. As if we were producing milk shakes, or maybe Margaritas. Blending of course sounds benevolent and gentle, and sometimes we were, but we were also extreme in our attempts to reconstruct our lives.

Patrick often says that being brought up in the seventies and eighties was like being brought up by wolves. Though, according to the Nature Channel, wolves seem to be model parents, given to acts of heroic self sacrifice to keep their cubs alive and well.

But Patrick's parents weren't anywhere near that noble. We didn't stalk caribou or small vermin, and he knew that we wouldn't give up our own lives for the good of the pack. We were more like fairy tale wolves, lying patiently in grandmother's bed, waiting to offer one more cracked plan. Just one more time. To make us blend, even if it killed us.

It all had to do with energy. How much to expend, how much to hold back. Ideally we should have let things happen naturally, but there was no "natural," not in the early days of a new family shakily forming and reforming.

One of our early experiments, our aborted sea urchin scheme, gives an indication of just how far we thought we needed to go to find our way home. The sea urchins also help to explain our disastrous need for Ben, how far we needed to go to save him and to save ourselves in the process.

It shouldn't have been so difficult. We were astonished in those early days to discover how good it was to be loving instead of fighting, to be sharing, laughing, and being sexy. Oh, none of these terms even come to the truth of it, but we were feeling fantastic.

Why couldn't it have stayed so simple? Maybe we were too complicated for our own good. Maybe we didn't know how to float on top of the good feelings. We needed to stay in charge—looking for trouble. We needed to know where we were going.

In the overheated real estate market of the eighties, our housing prospects were grim. Crowded together in the condo, we kept trying to figure how we could live together, at my place or his or in another space altogether. We spent too much time worrying about what would happen once the kids were all out of the house and on their own, but needing, all the same, a place they could return to.

And so we began driving around New England on the weekends, peering into real estate windows, scooping up brochures advertising houses for sale. We ended up spending a week in West Point, Maine, a fishing village near Bath.

This wasn't an accidental destination. David was getting antsy. Since law wasn't as exciting to practice as it had been to learn, he began reading and dreaming about something completely different: aquaculture. Not only did we love seafood, preferably raw, but we also loved to scuba dive. And sea urchin was our favorite food.

It wasn't that difficult for us to imagine owning a dock and working with a team of scuba divers who would harvest sea urchins. It wouldn't be easy; we knew that. I gave David a book on the lobster gangs of Maine that described in detail the closed and insular world of the lobstermen jealously guarding their lobster pots and their rights to locations you wouldn't want to invade.

"Those are lobstermen," he explained patiently. "Sea urchins are in a completely different market."

Japanese brokers were paying big money for the urchins, *uni* in Japanese. The apparently insatiable Japanese desire for *uni* encouraged a new generation of fishermen to turn to scuba diving to harvest the urchins by hand.

What surprised us was how easy it would have been to start up the urchin venture in 1988. If David had the money and energy to invest in the *uni* cowboys working the pier in West Point—tough and lean and sweet and friendly guys ready to dive into freezing water in their winter dry suits—they would be willing to work for him. They told us that, and I still believe them.

All we would need to do would be to build or buy a pier, buy a house, and set up an urchin station. All David would need to do was quit his job and work approximately twenty hours a day to start up the business. All I would need to do would be to commute the three hours each way between Tufts and West Point every week and stay over three nights in Somerville, unless I wanted to do the commute every day that I taught. Piece of cake.

We traveled back and forth about eight times that winter, testing the metaphorical waters. Not buying anything, but imagining what it would be like to live in the bleak and forbidding winter world of Maine. The days were cold and dark and dreary until they broke out suddenly into sublime beauty.

Sometimes the three-hour trip took four or five hours in snow-storms that would force us to the side of the road waiting out the blizzard. Roxie came along on those car trips, content to look out the window onto the stark landscape. She was our only fan. Our kids tried not to pay attention to what we were doing. Raised by wolves, they knew when to lie low.

We took out a subscription to the *Maine Times*, an alternative newspaper that presented a realistic picture of life on the rural maritime coast and in the more depressed, hardscrabble interior.

Around this time, a young wife and mother, Karen Wood, was accidentally shot and killed by hunters while she was hanging up wash in her own back yard. Hard line Mainers thought it was her own fault to be out and about in hunting season, wearing, of all things, white mittens and a brown scarf. She looked like a white tailed deer, some people said. Why wasn't she wearing orange? Everybody knew that you had to wear orange even in your back yard during hunting season.

We'd read the stories debating the pros and cons of the case, and we became uneasy. How could anybody think that a woman wearing white mittens and a brown scarf could be a justifiable target during hunting season?

Besides—guns. Guns gave me panic attacks.

170

But we still kept on driving back and forth on the weekends, leaving Boston early in the morning, returning exhausted late at night, imagining the perfect pier.

In early March, David angle parked on the main street of Brunswick, Maine, in front of a diner. He parked so badly that he banged his headlight into the bumper of the car next to us. The bumper was fine, but we had heard the ominous tinkle of glass from our shattered headlight.

"David," I asked, "have you ever been in even the smallest accident before today?"

David shook his head, in a state of shock.

"Never, you know that, for god's sake, you know I can park a goddamned car. Blindfolded."

"So, what do you think? Is this just too hard? Are we out of our minds? I mean, if you can't park because you're so tired, what am I going to be like driving back and forth to Tufts from West Point? You know how I park."

"I know," he said, "how you drive."

We lost our appetite. We didn't even get out of the car. David pulled back out of his parking place, and we drove back to Boston, neither of us saying a word until we left the state of Maine.

"Maybe," I said, safe in the darkness, "maybe we like things to be hard."

"Maybe," David said, "we're both nuts."

"Maybe," I said, "we can't handle being happy. Maybe we just need to work, too much, maybe…"

"Maybe," he said, "Maybe we can work harder at relaxing."

We laughed nervously.

We have never once returned to West Point—not even when the wild flowers covered the wetlands in glorious May and June. West Point meant a failure of the imagination and the spirit. We decided to confine our experience with sea urchins to Japanese restaurants, where we only order *uni* from Maine, and only during the months of November, December, January and February. March can be chancy.

We learned that much, but not enough to keep us from getting

Ben ten years later. Some things wouldn't change. We were still working hard to relax.

After Roxie died, I took aimless but frantic walks around the Arboretum, four, five miles at a time, up and down fairly predictable hills looking, I thought, for exercise. I had never been able to take such walks with Roxie. Indolent, unflappable, she would usually expire with the effort or, more likely, the boredom of getting as far as the lily ponds, barely one quarter of a mile from the main gate. But then, I had not loved her for her physical stamina, but for her extraordinary beauty.

I missed her with a terrible longing. I missed her stubborn sweetness, her solid, muscular body, I missed holding her, massaging her, running my fingers through her fur to release the dead hairs into the golden afternoon air. I even missed her occasional outrage when a sweet spot turned suddenly touchy, when in the middle of a rubdown, she would leap up, stare at me balefully, and stride out of the room.

But I did not miss dragging her around the pond and through the Arboretum. I tried to exult in the crazy cross country jaunts I took myself on, erratic attempts to get as much mileage as I could out of the 260-plus acres of the Arboretum. If you had filmed me from above, you would have thought me demented. Circling, reeling, scrambling up and down the same hill, up and down again, I lost scarves and keys and hats. I also pounced on dog walkers, boring them with stories about my poor dead dog.

I was not looking for another dog. David and I agreed on that. We had bought a cottage in Scotland in 1996, and we worried about UK Rabies Control. Xenophobic Brits would not allow animals into the country unless they were quarantined for six months. Rabies, it was presumed, ran rampant in other countries, while Britain, it was argued, remained rabies free.

Rules have since been relaxed and now animals from EU countries are given their own passports as well as microchips under their skins providing proof of their rabies vaccinations. There are finally plans to allow animals from the more barbaric continents, the Americas, Australia and New Zealand to get their own little passports, their own microchips. But in 1999, a relaxation of the Rabies laws seemed highly unlikely for those of us living in the colonies.

It made sense not to get another dog. Besides, I was getting older. A dog might live another 14 years. Did I really want to be dragging a dog up and down icy hills, or be dragged, more likely, when I was 68?

And by now, I knew that I was not that good with animals. I knew deep down that I had never really learned how to train a dog. Dixie had been too aggressive, Roxie oblivious to training, and as for Rosie, let us not forget her desire to please. She had trained herself overnight. I had, in truth, never made any impact upon any of the dogs. They remained essentially themselves, and I accommodated myself to whatever I thought was their nature.

But oh, that dog itch. As I pushed myself past the hemlocks of the Arboretum wilderness, as I made myself climb up Peter's Hill and down again, talking to myself, I was really spying on dogs, trying to imagine them mine. I had, I discovered, extremely high standards. Most dogs didn't appeal to me. They were too slavish or too remote, too slobbering or too haughty.

I decided against a big dog. Roxie had been almost 90 pounds, big enough to pull me down the front stairs if she took a notion. Once, after a particularly difficult conversation with my brother about our mother's Alzheimer's, I gave her a late night walk. We crept along the icy streets until she suddenly tugged on the leash and threw me into the air. I landed on my head, thinking of brain cells draining out into the snow. No, I couldn't handle a big dog, but I didn't like them small and yappy. I needed a medium sized dog. Not that I was getting a dog.

But I began dreaming of Border Collies. Every September, I visited a farm outside of Lincoln to collect "my" lamb, its tiny frozen legs carefully wrapped in butcher's paper, its chops, its liver and heart, its various more mysterious parts ground into one pound portions to be made into chili and bulgur pilaf.

The sheep grazing, the collies gazing, ever alert, and Betty, their breeder, training them to herd sheep, so splendid in her worn woolen jacket and her muddy wellies—all these sights fascinated me. I wanted that life even as I knew that I would never possess the discipline to manage it. Nonetheless, I began to explore the possibility of getting a puppy.

In September 1999, we had just returned from Scotland, where David and I watched sheep dogs drive wild sheep up and down the hills. Their powers of concentration daunted us. We wondered if they ever relaxed. At sheep dog trials, they stood in nervous readiness, staring hard at their shepherds, mostly elderly men dressed for the part in tweeds.

The collies' intensity both attracted and disturbed me. I stalked them in our wee town of Kirkcudbright, watching them watch their owners. They seemed to skitter sideways on leash, pulling slightly against their owners' intentions, with a purpose in mind that transcended their mundane surroundings. Let the Labs and Retrievers lazily and cheerfully float through the streets, let the Terriers sniff and burrow at the edges of the pavement. Collies were wrapped in their own sweet and serious concentration. They would occasionally glance up at their owners, eyes shining then with good will, grinning, like the wolf in Little Red Riding Hood with their long and lovely snouts.

I had talked to Betty many times about getting a Border Collie, but I was always worried about not being a good enough owner. A collie owner needed to be calm and consistent, energetic and patient. Oh, right.

This is where the safe should have fallen from the fifth floor window to flatten me into the ground. Instead, filled with impatient desire, I began signing over my future, promising to take puppy training, and vowing to develop a singularity of character that would miraculously emerge with the lessons.

David remained skeptical, maybe because he knew my character, but he also found himself attracted by the famous intelligence of the breed. This was before we both learned that intelligence could be deployed against our own needs and desires. We agreed, with a degree of terror, that we really wanted a collie. No other breed would do.

Even after talking to our friend Jesper about his collie's early habit of gnawing on the kitchen table and his continued nervousness approaching terror triggered by men wearing hats or carrying opened umbrellas, even after reading the bewildering tales of collie meltdown on the Border Collie rescue web sites, we put down a deposit on our puppy about to be born.

The puppies were born November 30, 1999, and David and I first visited them in late December. They were out of their whelping box and rolling around, continuous balls of motion and energy, all fur and baby fat, pushing yogurt containers around the floor and swatting at old sneakers hanging from a rope. Betty chose for us a sweet, cuddly dog that looked like his mother, in retrospect, the perfect pup. But David was attracted to a bold, prancing boy, handsome like his father with a pronounced blaze on his forehead and a charged gleam in his eyes.

I really wanted David to love the new dog and to make him his own. Roxie had been my dog, allowing David certain rights and privileges, but insisting upon an exclusive relationship with me alone that ultimately kept David away. This time I wanted him to share the dog, the walks and the training. That way the dog would be "ours," the surrogate child who would justify us and save us from ourselves.

Not that we were lonely. We were needy. Rhymes with greedy.

So we stuck to David's choice, also the choice of a bright and active couple probably in their late twenties full of energy and dog wisdom. They agreed to take instead the sweet and calm dog, and we brought dapper, rowdy Ben back to Jamaica Plain.

We chose the name because Ben means mountain in Gaelic. The name is appropriate. Ben, as big as a mountain, fundamentally turned our lives inside out. Bigger than Ben Lomond, as big as Ben Nevis, our mountain dog cried all the way home in the car, nipping me with his sharp baby teeth.

The puppy days blur. Ben tore through the hallway, ran into the living room, raced through the dining room, spun around the kitchen, and charged back again through the hall into the living room where I would be sitting on the couch, trying to read or write, waiting for him to lunge into the air at me, around me, onto the seat beside me, and then down again for another lap.

He housebroke himself in about fifteen minutes, triumphantly barking at the French door to be let out into the garden. Leaping down back steps, he ran in wide and joyous circles, plunging into the snow, skidding across the ice, and hiding under the porch steps where he proceeded to dig up clods of frozen dirt to emerge full of mud and snow.

In again, out again, all the day into the night, Ben ran rampant, collapsing only occasionally for a brief fifteen minute nap. I fumbled around, clumsily trying to exert some sort of control, practicing *Come* and *Sit*. My commands were frantic calls for help.

"Sit, sit, sit," I would say, breaking the first rule of dog training: Never give a command twice.

Okay, then, *Sit. Settle.*

I guess not.

Instead, Ben herded me up and down the stairs, nipping at my ankles, making holes in all of my socks. He was a nimble learner and quickly made a habit of racing me to the bathroom, following me in, standing with great glee to see that I was actually getting ready to sit on the toilet, *Sit* Carol, and then, certain all was secure, he would tear out the door, leaving me discreetly, to my own devices. This became a major job for Ben, the one act of herding that he performed with great and serious pleasure.

Maybe we were too serious, and maybe we were too old. Certainly David and I worked too hard to be perfect. I see people with puppies now and think that the best are the most casual, easy in letting their puppy follow them along off leash, certain that their animal will not fling itself into the ongoing traffic. We learned in Puppy School to never, no never let the dog off leash until he came when called.

Come when called? Yes, no, it depended. For months we kept Ben leashed, dragging him—and us—up and down muddy hills and banks to give him the hours of exercise he needed. But in truth, we were the ones who were leashed, the ones that Ben drove around the Arboretum and into the pond, bounding and straining. We spent hours flinging green tennis balls in and out of the living room and back out into the garden trying to wear him out. We also played hide and seek, calling out to Ben to find us huddled inside closets, and he always won, grinning and wagging his feathery tail.

He didn't like dancing. Over the years, David and I had done a mean tango, a less adventurous rumba and, always, at the end, a slow clutch from the living room into the dining room through the kitchen and back again to Frank Sinatra and Piazzola and the Buena Vista Social Club, late into the night.

Roxie had indulged us in our harmless pursuits, occasionally leaping up to hug us as we careened around the living room. But our dancing outraged Ben. He would throw his squirmy body at us, bark sharply, and nip at our heels when he landed back on his. David said that he was a Scottish Presbyterian dog.

Worse still, Ben had no tolerance for sex. In the early days, Ben was "crated." Crating had become the new and efficient way of dealing with dogs home alone. The puppy trainer, her name was God, told us to keep Ben in a very large crate at night, and when we were out of the house. He settled into his pseudo cave quite happily, burrowing into the rugs and toys, happy that is until we made love.

Even after shutting our bedroom door, even after carefully closing the door to the TV room, where the crate and Ben lived, even after playing Brahms First Symphony quite loudly on the CD player, even after putting Babe on the VCR, where all of those darling mechanical Border Collies pranced around for his entertainment, Ben would bark to raise the dead when we approached orgasm. This was a dog that you could not fool. He knew the moment when the rhythm became deep and clear, no matter how quiet we tried to be. Then he'd start in, barking with frantic urgency, stopping only when we finished.

Ben frustrated us with his craziness, but he also cracked us up. We would often end up laughing, howling, and yelling at him to pipe down. Just as often, we would often end up on the third floor barricaded behind the closed door of our guest room, still able to hear his sharp, nervous bark. Was he celebrating us or chastising us? Or was he joining in?

He was, David said, a Scottish Presbyterian dog with a deep crazy streak. How deep we would learn in time.

Well, at least I learned—finally—how to train a dog. Some years later, after we gave Ben to Jennifer (do not worry, Ben is not in doggy heaven accepting no visitors, but happily living in New Hampshire with the owner of the kennel he visited so many times) David and I took a trip to Cooperstown, New York, where we met our good friends from Buffalo, Jerry and Judy.

Judy and I were hiking above the town when we passed a farm. Trees turning red, wisps of smoke rising lazily from a bonfire halfway up the mountain, gray-white farmhouse peeling a little, but what a front porch wrapped around sinking foundations. We were taking the perfect country walk, until a Rottweiler came barreling out of his yard into the road and began barking at us. We walked on with determination, imagining that the dog would tire once he realized that we weren't going to trespass, but he followed us down the road, showing his teeth and slobbering. Suddenly he began to lunge at us, barking wildly. Walking briskly wasn't doing the trick.

I stopped, looked down at him, not making eye contact, and said firmly, Sit. Once.

The dog did, promptly, looking a little startled.

Go home, I commanded. Once.

The dog turned tail, literally, and ran back into his yard, no doubt recognizing that he was toast.

It had only taken two years of dog lessons, $4,500 of fees for behavior modification therapy, dog psychology, and clicker training to teach me how to say Sit only once and mean it.

"Damn, you're good," Judy said. Oh yeah.

Puppy school had its virtues. The dogs got to run around off leash and socialize. Ben became fast friends with a German shepherd. He ran circles around him. There were three Border Collies in the class, one the sweet and adaptable brother to Ben that our breeder wanted us to take home. Oddly, the siblings demonstrated little interest in each other. Fly, the dog we rejected, performed brilliantly every week, coming, sitting, staying, you name it. Ben fared not so well. He seemed to be bursting with an energy that could not be disciplined. But then, we were not good disciplinarians, particularly me. I was probably the worst student in the puppy class, freezing, clutching and repeating my commands.

"Once, Carol, once, got it? Once!" shouted the puppy trainer, violating her own command. But David wasn't that much better. In those early days of training, Ben's lack of focus unsettled us, particularly when the other owners would praise the virtues of the breed. Collies are so smart, we'd hear, as we watched Ben creep sideways looking for a handy escape route.

Ben was so smart that he started to bark and shake with fear, or was it displeasure, when we even approached the car to drive him to puppy class every Wednesday night. Our dog was so smart that he could tell the time and the day of the week. Wednesday at 7:30 became "Time of Infamy." I suppose in retrospect one of the reasons for his terror of the relatively easygoing class was that on a fundamental level, it thwarted him.

For eventually I did learn how to keep him from lunging at me and nipping me on my arms and legs, making holes in my sweaters and pants and easily punctured skin. Before we'd been to puppy class, a friend at school gave me weekly arm tests, checking the nip marks. I felt like an abused wife, the sort who wears long sleeves to hide her bruises. Staring at the scabs, he just sighed, and then asked the important question: Why would I accommodate myself to the needs of an animal that was hurting me?

Oh, I knew why, I'd been in therapy for five years to answer the question, but what to do with the knowledge? Somehow the answer didn't save me from my passionate attachment to Ben the nipper. I let Ben hurt me because he got my attention. And the pain was familiar, old pain reminding me that I had to be better. But the short answer is, of course, too simple.

Puppy class was designed to teach me how to protect myself from the lunge attacks, and it did. We learned how to keep Ben on the floor, off the couch, at our feet, down, down, down, like a dog. And he didn't like that one bit. He thought he was a mountain, not a dog.

When he felt like it, Ben could perform the tricks of the puppy trade with style and grace. He was particularly good at navigating the obstacle courses, weaving his way around the cones placed between him and the goal line. Agility training, that's what he needs, the puppy trainers said. It would only take all of our weekend time, and two or three nights during the week, but he deserved it. Fly's owners were driving all the way to Hingham to learn agility, and we could see the results—Fly flew.

We groaned. It seemed impossible. David was lawyering and learning about the dot-com world while I was teaching and writing, and both of us were trying to spend time with our kids. Molly's Caitlin was eight months old when we got Ben. Patrick and Kari, Molly, John and Caitlin all lived close by. How could we spend weekends in Hingham and Scituate and Wellfleet doing agility? We had to make pancakes and take Caitlin to JP Licks in her stroller.

The theory was that Ben would accommodate himself to those outings, but that's another story. The short version: leaping, lunging, nipping, Ben terrified Molly. She didn't want him anywhere near Caitlin, Caitlin whose third or fourth word was Doggy. Doggy. Doggy. Doggy. Ben was just one more sign of our treacherous hearts.

During his final class, Ben demonstrated his gleeful disdain for the entire enterprise. In the great obstacle race, he managed to knock over all of the orange cones, careened sideways into the folding chairs and came in second to last, behind the sweet, clumsy German shepherd, Ben's best friend.

The puppies were duly rewarded. The most obedient received giant rawhide bones, the lowest and the least were given bandanas that said puppy graduate. Ben wore his home in the car, not barking. We were, after all, going away from school, not towards it. Ben didn't know it then, but there would be more school.

The puppy trainers urged us to sign on for more training. "A Border Collie should not be the second worst puppy in the class," the assistant said, trying not to smirk. "Ben is capable of so much more."

The new trainer, tough, burly, a regular marine sergeant, sold us all pinch collars that first night, a requirement of the course.

A few words about leashes and collars. The collar is a relatively simple device that goes around the neck of the animal, good for displaying the dog's license and rabies tag, and of course the ideal place to attach the leash. Snap leash onto collar and walk smartly down the street with obedient dog.

But if, and this happens often, if the dog does not want to walk smartly, but would rather drag the walker at his own pace, the standard leash/collar arrangement can fail, and can become on an icy or slippery day lethal. A squirmy dog like Ben can wiggle out of his collar altogether, leaving walker with empty collar, useless leash and loose dog charging down the street. One then turns to various solutions.

There is the choke collar, made of fabric, leather, or chain, with a loop on each end. Place one loop into the other, pull, attach your leash to the second loop, and you have made yourself an effective collar that tightens around the neck of the recalcitrant dog with one snap of your wrist. Akitas have necks thick as tree trunks, defended with two thick and heavy layers of hair, but even they responded to the pull of the choke, in their own negligent Akita way. Ben's bony neck is the size of my wrist, unprotected by his wavy, silky hair that flowed rather than matted over his neck. To choke him was to torture him. We didn't use the choke.

But the standard collar/leash arrangement didn't seem to work either. Ben squirmed out of his collar three or four times in the Arboretum, sending us up and down the hills commanding him to come. Enter the pinch collar, constructed of a series of interlocking stainless steel prongs that literally pinch the neck. One must be careful to attach the pinch collar next to the collar, not over it, or the pinch will not be hard enough to get the dog's attention. This is harder than it sounds. The dog naturally resists the entire procedure, wiggling and thrusting to keep the pinchers away from soft and vulnerable skin.

But let's say that finally the pinch collar has been laid professionally upon the dog neck. That accomplished, walker gives one sharp yank on the leash, dog feels pinch, and decides to behave. Pinch collar enthusiasts argue that the collar is more humane because it only takes one pinch for discipline to be asserted. One pinch, they say, is not as dangerous as a concerted attack on the windpipe by a choke collar.

If the pinch collar fails, walker can resort to even more devices, complicated harnesses sometimes involving the nose of the dog, sometimes just the main body of the dog. As a last resort, remote control instruments can zap the animal into submission. You can find all of these items at your nearest pet store, and probably many more since I last made a visit—all invented to make the dog walk with the Walker.

You can imagine how much Ben hated the pinch collar. We used it off and on for six weeks in early summer, beautiful lush days around the pond, up and down Peter's Hill, reverting back as often as we could to the old leash/collar arrangement until it would once again fail us and I'd find myself chasing Ben off leash up and down Hemlock Hill.

But God, those days were beautiful. Lush isn't nearly the right word for the Arboretum that May. Once, finally run out of energy, Ben sat ecstatic in the middle of a field of wild flowers, his head peeking out of daisies and buttercups. I brought my camera the next day but, by then, the field had been mowed.

The second level dog training felt like boot camp, no puppy socializing, just militaristic exercises that Ben rejected. Ben forgot most willfully every command he had ever learned and began lunging again, angrily. Didn't we see, he seemed to ask, what we were doing to him? We were reading dog books filled with contradictory advice, but all agreed on one thing: we had to be the boss. Border Collie sites on the web were telling us that we were doomed. The battle was already over, and we did not deserve such a dog.

Meanwhile, Ben and I made many dog friends in the Arboretum and at the pond. While our dogs frisked, howled, lurched, and hid out, we owners, we the actual "owned," talked honestly about our struggles. We were not alone, and that knowledge brought solace.

Even now, as I walk through Jamaica Plain, wandering around the pond and into the Arboretum, I can see an army of dog walkers bearing harnesses and collars, carrying whistles and electronic zappers, clickers and treats, squirt guns and balls, going forth to battle their dogs' natures and their own. They cry out for obedience, for relief, for forgiveness, for love—dogs and caretakers together—high sharp Yorkie sopranos, deep baying Bloodhound basses, seductive Whippet mezzos, teasing Border Collie tenors and, of course, the humans, barking out the recitative: *Sit, Stay, Come,* all center stage players in the Doggy Opera.

I write now of Ben's body—flesh and blood driven by a restless and indomitable spirit. Border Collies like Ben, registered with the Border Collie Association, come in all sizes. They are not bred for conformation, but for work. AKC registered collies are altogether different, bred to "show," as in Show Dog. Ben is a mid-sized dog, weighing forty to forty five pounds, with a surprisingly muscular chest, skinny legs that almost seem to bend, making him able to walk and run aslant, a long, swishy tail that feathers up when he is happy, and disappears between his legs when he gets nervous. All sinew and nerve, he can run for hours without stopping.

Once he demonstrated his maniacal hardiness by dashing up and down the mountain paths of the Rocky Woods on a deeply slashed front paw. We had no idea that the paw had been cut until we got back to the car and saw the blood. We drove immediately to the vet's, where he received stitches and an Elizabethan cone collar that he destroyed overnight in his crate.

His white snout, his white blaze, his white chest, his white boots, even the white tip of his tail never held dirt. The Teflon kid, Ben could roll exultantly in mud, in sand, and be radiantly clean by the time we returned home from a walk. I never knew how.

Shit was something different, stopping even his recuperative powers, but oh how he loved to roll in it deep in the thickets up in the hill over the pond. Then he needed to be hosed down, washed, brushed, Herculean tasks, which I tried to circumvent by taking him into the pond. One morning the Park Ranger busted me, sending me home after a ten-minute lecture about the Boston reservoir system. A small price, I thought, to avoid washing and brushing Ben who hated the brush and comb.

Even when he was full grown, Ben could squeeze under the sofa in search of a ball. It's almost as if he could collapse his skeletal structure. When we played hide and seek, he managed to press his already skinny body under the bed, behind the door, or lying flat under the blankets, becoming literally invisible. You could imagine him then, supine on a hillside in Scotland, beady eyes peering out from his wolf-like face, watching the sheep. He knew how to make himself disappear, a talent invaluable in the Arboretum when he saw a dog that he didn't want to encounter. Ben was no fighter, and while he seemed to enjoy the company of most dogs, he also knew how to stand sideways against a tree to hide from the dreaded bloodhound that went after anything on four legs, or from the incorrigible Corgi twins.

Ben's body was almost always moving, except when he slept. Roxie had spent hours on the Turkish rug in front of the fireplace, stretched out on her side, monumentally peaceful. Individual hairs seemed to shine in the sunlight. Ben saw the rug as something to chew on, tease, and push around the living room. He preferred the couch, and we were stupid enough to let him lie there, on his back, four feet waving lazily in the air, his skinny, hairy body, his neutered private parts shockingly exposed to our view, our touch. He grinned in his sleep. Sometimes we let him sleep with us in our bed.

That's right. Stop right here and read that sentence again. We violated the biggest taboo. Every trainer told us that dogs belong on the floor or in the crate, but never ever on the bed. But oh the feeling of squirmy Ben at peace, Ben between David and me, sometimes wriggled up on my pillow, one paw on my shoulder. In bed, he became quiet at last, nuzzling us, kissing us until he fell into a short sleep punctuated by sighs and whimpers. He was so warm and soft, sometimes in the summer almost too hot to touch. But his nose was always cold when he nuzzled us in his sleep.

I am looking at a picture of Ben that I snapped through the screen door. He is standing on the front porch staring out at me on the steps holding the camera. His black silky ears are partially erect, his brown eyes are snapping with eager delight. His eyes say it all, not mournful and compassionate, the way brown eyes usually seem, but sharp and clear, the eyes of a challenger. He is grinning, white teeth gleaming. He looks as if he wants to jump through the screen and bite me.

It was time to neuter Ben. Dr. Groper urged us to do so when he turned six months. Harboring no illusions about keeping his masculinity intact, we made an appointment for mid-June, one week after my brother was scheduled to visit. Tom and Kat and the three boys were driving from Chicago, and would stop with us on their trip through the northeast. We were excited about seeing them, but also worried about Ben.

"One thing," I said, "please don't bring Louisa." I explained about Ben, about his unpredictable nature, his about to be neutered aggression. Louisa is a Shetland Sheep Dog, impeccably ladylike, fonder of people than dogs.

"She won't like Ben," I said, "he's too jumpy; he'll get into her face."

"I don't know," Tom said, "I just don't know; Louisa hates being in a kennel."

"She'll hate Ben even more," I kept insisting, and he finally agreed, no Louisa.

They arrived with Louisa. We understood, knowing how impossible it was to not give in to a dog's needs. Louisa hated being in a kennel. There were no other options. Besides, Louise was a sweetheart, a regular little Lassie. Dancing on her hind legs, she could have been a circus dog, a circus dog with reserve. Ben bounded, pranced, sashayed. She swished her tail, stepped primly away from him, giving him an occasional nip to suggest that he keep his distance. Her aloofness seemed to attract the leaping Romeo. Ben made more overtures, bumping into her side, circling her. Louisa bared her teeth. Ben barked. Doggy Tango.

It turned out that Louisa was going into heat.

Louisa was going into heat, Ben's testosterone was kicking in, and my nephews wanted to sightsee. It's hard to sightsee with a dog. A very intrepid family, they managed to bring Louisa on trips to Concord, Lexington and Crane beach. But since you couldn't walk a dog onto the Constitution, I found myself staying home with the two nervous, circling dogs. We had tried to separate them, crating Ben, leaving Louisa the run of the house, but Ben, smelling her presence, barked. By now, you know about his barks. Louisa would bark back in a higher range. It was impossible not to laugh and not to get a headache.

The plan was that I would watch the dogs, walk the dogs, crate Ben, shut Louisa up in the third floor bedroom, and meet everybody in the North End for dinner. Walk the dogs. What I should have done, I know now, was crate Ben, walk Louisa, then lock up Louisa and walk Ben.

What I really should have done, I know now, was lock the dogs in separate rooms on the third floor, take the T to South Station, hop on a bus to Woods Hole, and sail to Martha's Vineyard where I could take a taxi to The Black Dog in Oak Bluffs. That was a dog I could manage, iconic, static, docile. Get your tee shirt for $14.95.

But instead, I got out their leashes, and they both started in, lobbying, protesting and resisting. They barked and strutted, snapped and barked again, and, finally, fell onto each other in a real down and out dogfight. As I have already said, Ben is no fighter and Louisa seemed to be aloof, but now, all bets were off. This was a tango turned into the world's middleweight championship.

I moved in to separate them. "Bad dogs," I shouted, unheard or at least disregarded. Ben was showing his teeth and lunging at Louisa who was striking back with her fierce forepaws. I reached down to grab him by his collar, and then it happened. Ben, eyes rolling, starting to froth at the mouth, Ben maddened, struck at my right arm. Then he went for the left.

Now, I had been nipped before, I had scabs to prove it, but this attack was different. Blood flowed freely from the bites. They weren't severe enough to be stitched, I could see that, but they were open and jagged, and there were just too many of them. I let go of Ben's collar. Louisa jumped onto the couch, out of the way. Ben whimpered, licking me, knowing that he had gone too far. I just kept looking at the blood dripping down my arm, onto the rug. I wasn't going to make it to the restaurant.

I bandaged up my arms, put Louisa on the third floor, and waited for everybody to come home. Ben would be no trouble tonight, I knew, abjection oozed out of him onto the rug. But I couldn't imagine what we would do next. The visit ended quickly. David had been teaching the boys how to play cribbage and presided over one last round with them that night. The next morning, they were off to Maine for lobsters. I felt embarrassed and confused (feelings that haunt me even now).

That visit was the last chance I had to be with Kat. I would next see her in the hospital the following October, where she lay in a coma, about to die of an aneurysm. She was forty-one years old. I remembered how she had glowed in the summer light, years before, on that night on the beach near Newburyport. She was pregnant with Joe and planning her future, the whole world before her.

"Are you out of your mind," Molly yelled. "Get rid of that dog, oh my god, Ma, you're too much. You think I'm bringing Caitlin to your house as long as Ben is around? Remember, remember when he jumped up and nipped her. I was holding her in my arms."

"He made a little hole in her sock," I said.

"Oh right, he didn't break the skin. I guess he's learned how to do that now. Look at your arms. What's wrong with you anyway?"

Patrick agreed with Molly. He thought that Ben was crazy, and particularly resented the way that the dog would lunge at his balls with his forelegs.

"I should wear a codpiece," he said, not really kidding.

My arms, no kidding about them, were signs of a craziness that was downright dangerous. It would be wrong, he argued, to keep such an aggressive and crazy dog.

Most people agreed with him.

But David and I, driven by desire and guilt, felt responsible for Ben's nature. We believed we had somehow created his defects, and we were willing to do anything to save him. You could say we were mad—small scale Dr. Frankensteins.

First we called the puppy trainer. She had known Ben early on; she'd know what to do. We drove to her home in Waltham. Ben had been barking so maniacally down Route 128 that he was actually losing his voice. We could barely get him out of the car. The trainer gave him the usual commands that he not only ignored but parodied. He slunk; he crawled; he crept on tiny collie feet, almost floating.

"The dog," she said, "is not acting like a dog at all." Ben was lying flat, pressing all of his flesh down into the ground, more like a punctured tire than an animal.

"You need to go back to the breeder," she said. "This dog's defective, genetically. There's no training that will change this sort of behavior."

Ben groaned, and sank further down into the grass, effacing himself and his doggy nature. We dragged him back into the car, where he proceeded to find his voice and bark sharply at such a high pitch that the trainer yelled as we pulled out of the driveway, "How can you stand it?"

We stood it because he would kiss us and nuzzle us and hug us with his little arms, and because he played the best ball that I have ever seen a dog play. But I am simplifying our emotions. I was also frightened of his sharp teeth. My arms were taking a long time to heal. I would look at the gouges and wonder just what we were doing? How could we stand it?

We visited the breeder. She thought that Ben was simply acting the way a pent up Border Collie will act when he isn't let off the leash. He needed to be free to run, she insisted, and she gave us the names of dog-friendly state parks where we could let Ben off the leash.

"But what if he doesn't come back," I asked.

"He'll have to," she said with determination. All we needed was a long, stout rope—forty yards or so. We spent many afternoons struggling with the awkward, heavy rope trying to make Ben come.

Here was the drill: attach the rope to Ben's collar, throw a ball out onto the field near the pond, call out to him once, "Come to me," and when he doesn't come, yank him back. Tug of war, only we needed more players on our side. We called and yanked and called and yanked. The exercise bore little relationship to the reality of Ben out and about, running up and down the hills, but we were eager to do anything that meant not giving up.

Dr. Groper was skeptical. He'd known Roxie, every epileptic particle of her, and had been amused at first that the dear, deaf Akita was being replaced with an unruly Border Collie. "You obviously like extremes," he said.

He didn't, however, find the state of my arms funny at all. "Look," he said, "you need a serious intervention here. A behaviorist would be some sort of help."

I asked about medication.

"For you or Ben?" he asked.

Doggy Prozac would not solve anything he said, and doggy Valium would be even worse.

"Listen," he said, "if Ben is aggressive, and I think he is, you don't want him relaxed. The reason he didn't bite deep into your arms is because he's developed inhibitions. He knows that he shouldn't hurt you. But if you take the edge off Ben, he wouldn't mind digging down deep and doing serious damage. No, you don't want this guy relaxed."

Ben stared at him fiercely, wanting to pace around the room. The vet outstared him and laughed to see Ben settle.

That was one of the commands in puppy school. *Settle. Settle,* Ben, only once.

Just say it once. *Settle.*

We went to an animal behaviorist where we learned several important things. First: the diagnosis. Dominance Aggression. And I was the object of that diagnosis. Ben had never nipped David, had he? Only me. Hand written after that diagnosis, I have the paper before me, is the prognosis: "guarded." A list follows, first a disclaimer noting that we have decided to keep Ben knowing the risks involved. Then the training tips, and they were plentiful and worthy. Nothing, we learned, in life, is free. Sitting in the behaviorist's office, I began to calculate the cost of Ben.

The behaviorist sat there, glowing, a darling young woman who could charm the most recalcitrant of animals into good behavior as long as they remembered that nothing in life was free. Ben would get nothing at all from us without sitting, staying, or doing a down. Open the door, throw him a ball, offer him food, put on his leash, take him for a walk, but only if he would sit, go down, stay, settle.

Say it once. Just once, Carol. Sit, down, stay, settle. No good doggy, no praise, just sit, down, stay, settle.

Much of her advice helped us. She taught us how to get Ben used to the brush and the comb. We plied him with liver treats and cheese to lure him into a relatively docile state.

First put the brush before him. Treat. Then move the brush closer to him. Treat.

Then pick up the brush and gesture towards him with the bristles. Treat. Finally, take a short, gentle stroke. Treat.

No excited enthusiastic cries reinforcing behavior. I was, it seemed, far too vocal, verging on the hysterical, in my encounters with Ben. No excitement. Just go easy, easy, treat, sit, treat, settle, treat, down, treat, stay.

Avoid confrontations, avoid excitement, down, Carol, stay, Carol. Settle.

Even the behaviorist was baffled by Ben's fanatical performance in the car. She loaned us a citronella collar. When Ben barked in the car, barked for that matter anywhere, he would trigger the collar to release a spray of citronella into the air. When this happened, we all received mild jolts of lemony fragrance, the sort of smell that you sometimes encounter in a rest room, not exactly disgusting, but certainly not appealing.

Theoretically, dogs hated the smell of citronella; even a whiff of it would make them stop barking. Ben barked; lemon spray filled the car; Ben barked; more lemon leaked out, gagging us; Ben barked; we sneezed; Ben barked; we coughed; Ben barked, emptying at last the collar of its precious fluid. And Ben barked some more.

Probably the behaviorist's best advice was to put Ben in a kennel. We had planned to go to Scotland for the month of August, but were worried about leaving Ben. Because, of course, we were so good for Ben. He'd miss us.

The behaviorist just laughed. "You all need a break," she said. "He's probably as tired of you as you are of him. A kennel just might turn him around."

I visited six of them in two days, Ben barking up and down Massachusetts and New Hampshire. Most of the kennels hygienic, air-conditioned, concrete bunkers, reminded me of the assisted living residences that we had explored when my mother started to succumb to her Alzheimer's. The walls of the kennels were painted the same soothing peach color. Too bad that dogs are color blind, I thought.

Animals were exercised fifteen minutes in the morning and fifteen minutes in the afternoon. This meant that somebody took them out on a leash into a common area, where they were left for ten minutes to socialize with their traumatized companions. You could hear them howling, those exercised animals, as you pulled into the driveway.

I knew that Ben would go out of his mind in such close and sanitized quarters. It was becoming hopeless until the breeder called. She had found the name of a good kennel, she said, and she spoke the truth.

The kennel saved us, or rather Jennifer, the kennel owner, did. She owned ten acres in New Hampshire, three of them fenced-in, for her seven dogs and six horses. Her dog boarders ran free inside three fenced in acres for hours at a time. The horses fascinated Ben. He stood next to them in the pond, never getting in over his knees, just chilling. Jennifer's voice is high pitched, urgent, and loving. She ruled from the first moment she said, "sit," only once, and Ben did, adoring her.

"He's crowding you," she said, "don't let him push at you; you've got to be in charge; make him keep his distance."

Ben grinned.

"Stay," she commanded. And he did.

All I needed to be was Jennifer. All it would take was a character transplant.

Fall 2000, all systems go. We were gearing up for our new life with Ben. When we came back from Scotland and picked Ben up from the kennel, we were stunned by his improvement. Buff, taut, every muscle exercised, he looked like a marine from Parris Island boot camp.

Okay, I thought, this is it. No leash: just Ben and David and me and the ball. And the leash of course to get him from our house on Prince Street over the Riverway, four lanes of determined traffic, and across Parkman Drive where cars wouldn't stop for elephants let alone women with dogs.

We had two particular destinations, our two private mountains, one in the Arboretum and the other one on Jamaica Pond. When I visit them now, they seem absurdly small, hillocks really, but there was a time when they were sacred spaces of great power, those places where we played our deadly serious game. The Arboretum hill was the best because it was out of sight.

Park Rangers rode their jeeps up and down the roads looking for dogs off leash. Sometimes they wrote tickets, but mostly they just reminded dog walkers of their civic obligations. "Where's your leash," they'd yell out the window. Grown men and women crept and crawled under bushes and thickets to keep out of the Rangers' sight. It wasn't pretty.

But in our ball space, a hill hidden behind the cork trees, just before you could veer off to the left into the mountainous area, we were free to run wild.

Here's what we did. I would stand at the top of the hill and throw the ball down to Ben, who would bound after it, retrieve it, and then carry it up to the top of the hill. By then, I would have scrambled to the bottom, ready to catch what he threw.

The dog could really throw, rotating that green tennis ball between his teeth, and tossing it into the air. The dog had aim, strength, and nerve. He could have been a contender.

Catching the ball, I'd clamber back up the hill, Ben would run back down, and we would continue our obsessive version of catch and throw. Dogs would come by, a Whippet named Felix, who could actually outrun him, Ben's particular favorite, and then a Puerto Rican street dog wearing a tee shirt, (he couldn't stand the cold) and finally an English Sheep Dog who liked to sit on Ben and lick his face. Ben was always happy to roll around and play with them, riotously, joyfully, but he was just as eager to get back to business, back to playing ball.

Occasionally I would try to entice him into rockier and more interesting terrains, but whenever I threw the ball up into the mountain (hill, really ... more precisely, a bump) on our left, he'd bring the ball resolutely back to the top of the hill, our hill, the only place worth standing upon in the Arboretum.

The Jamaica Pond hill was even less extraordinary to the unbiased eye. It rose from a hollow to overlook the water. There, I could run up and down, throwing and catching, while Ben fielded and pitched. We drew crowds, sometimes as many as ten people standing on the walkway looking down into our basin to watch Ben play baseball.

"That dog can throw," I'd hear, "look at that sucker, look at him field that ball!"

Because by now Ben was grandstanding, dancing, prancing, and loving the action. Dogs would move in and out of the neighborhood. Molly, the Bernese Mountain dog was the most significant visitor—she and Ben were truly, I think, for six months at least, in love—rolling across the dead leaves, pushing each other into the pond, licking each other all over. He also spent a lot of time with Felix, another Felix, an Australian Cattle Dog, even more high strung than Ben, who could catch Frisbees and balls with exquisite precision for hours at a time. Ben didn't do Frisbee. Not ever. He'd watch the disc fly past him with supreme indifference, while he waited for the ball, ball, ball.

After ball, we'd run down the ridge to the pond's edge. Labs and Goldens would be leaping and splashing, going after balls, floats, Frisbees, and even stones. Ben would tip toe after them, thrashing in the water, but he'd never go over his head. One particular Lab used to bound into the water after his ball, retrieve it, and then swim back to Ben up to his neck in the water to drop the ball before him. Ben would scoop it up into his mouth, charge back to shore, and turn finally back towards the Lab waiting in the water. Then Ben would throw the ball back to his tag team partner.

They could do this for hours on hot, lazy Indian summer afternoons, on foggy fall mornings, as the clear water rippled against the shore, as the geese flew overhead, as the leaves turned color and drifted into the pond.

Even the Ranger didn't mind, and occasionally stood on the ridge to watch their game. We lived in a small world, then, one that took up about a quarter of an acre, but a lot was going on in it.

David rejected my habitual and mechanical groove. "You're boring that dog to death, he said. To correct my obsessive mistakes, he took Ben on entirely different walks up and down the hills, into the Hemlock plantations, over Peter's Hill and back again. He threw the ball to drive Ben forward, refusing to stop for the games of catch and pitch that Ben exacted from me, and he succeeded. He made Ben act like a dog, still obsessive, still manic but recognizably canine.

Things seemed almost normal, but the normality was uneasily created in a year of terrible abnormality. For in late October, Kat died and the world changed entirely. We made trips back to Chicago to be with Tom and the boys, Futile gestures, really. The painful blankness, the heaviness in the heart could not be lightened.

But I am talking now of Ben and in the world of Ben, peace shakily reigned. He'd stopped nipping, sat on command, and had almost dropped his irritating habit of jumping on people, even though he still stalked the car, that great object of fear and desire. Walking down the front steps became perilous, as Ben strained on his leash, desperate to reach the Saab. He'd jump up then, onto the door and begin to whimper. Once inside, sitting on the back seat, he would regain his dignity, but as soon as the car started, he would bark sharply, producing a high, nervous, excruciating sound.

Getting Ben out of the car was almost impossible; he'd snarl and snap, resisting threats, lures, and treats. We kept him on his leash whenever he was in the car, shutting the door on the end of the leash, allowing it to stick out. When it was time to get Ben out of the car, we would grab the leash, open the door, and yank.

One spring day, he jumped through an open car window onto a neighbor's front seat, refusing to leave. David had to lure him out with liver treats. To cure the barking, we tried doggy seatbelts, crates, classical music, and once again, we bought him a citronella collar.

We even bought a second car, a little Daewoo, because of its hatchback. We had the crazy notion that Ben would like standing in the hatchback, and that the Daewoo would make him feel more secure.

We planned to use the car to take Ben on adventures, to the Blue Hills, to the Rocky Woods. And we did, Ben barking all the way, until he split his paw almost in two scrambling against the metal runner that held up the back seat of the car in his struggle to gain mastery over us, over himself, over the car.

After four weeks of Ben struggling to get out of yet another Elizabethan collar (more like a lamp shade, each replacement costing fifteen dollars), we pretty much gave up the road trips. Ben's life became circumscribed by the areas I could reach on foot. I've never been in better shape in my life.

I remember hearing a radio broadcast long ago describing all of the disasters accompanying a severe Nor'easter. Trees crashed down, live wires covered the streets, and basements flooded.

But then a sad and strange story filled the air. A Border Collie had run out into the storm and was feared to be lost. His owners were worried that he wouldn't be able to find his way home. He had not been out of the house for seven years. Not been out of the house? I remember wondering what kind of monsters could his owners be? Didn't they understand that collies needed exercise? What were they thinking? How had that poor dog survived?

But that was before Ben. For in the fall of 2001, Ben began melting down so insistently, that I could imagine him becoming that mad dog in the attic.

We still don't understand what went so wrong. Should we have stopped going to Scotland? I spent June there and then came home, leaving David behind, so that I could be with Ben in July. Ben had been in New Hampshire and, as always, glowed with health and energy after a month in the country.

His coat shone, glossy, silky; even his teeth looked whiter.

But July was a minor disaster. Instead of overestimating my importance to Ben that summer, I should have stayed in Scotland and let him be. For back in JP, Ben was beginning to develop what would become an insurmountable problem. He was becoming hypersensitive to urban noises.

Urban isn't quite the right word. Anything mechanical would do the trick. The Arboretum was constructing an elaborate shrub garden, not far from our hill. Builders were digging up land and erecting stonewalls, "dry stane dykes" they'd be called in Scotland. The slightest noise from the construction site set Ben off. Back up beeps from the trucks, the sound of rocks crashing, the whine of a chain saw, all these things terrified him. He would freeze, he would slink and, finally, he would bolt.

I got to know too well the sounds of that summer, the truck brakes moaning, sirens screeching, alarms ringing, the gears grinding. Sometimes I could even predict them. Like Ben, I was becoming hypersensitive and, even now, when I hear the sound of back-up warning beepings, I clutch.

We live in a noisy place, I know, but when we were at Jamaica Pond, I would study the other dogs jumping and splashing in the water. Not one of them froze in terror at the sound of the garbage truck; not one turned suddenly to run across the Riverway all the way home. Only Ben did that. The vet thought that the problem was neurological, a hard-wired one. It was hard to see how behavior modification could allay such terror.

Garbage days were the worst.

Monday at around six in the morning, Ben would sit on my head, burrowing into me and into the pillow and he would start to shake. I would try to soothe him, unsuccessfully, not even able to hear yet what he dreaded.

But I knew that approximately twenty minutes away, the recycling truck was heading for our street and I knew that Ben could already hear its crashing and banging and whining. And somewhere about thirty minutes away, the garbage truck followed.

Beep beep beep went its back-up warning, driving right into Ben's brain. He would shake and cry in anticipation, but when the trucks actually appeared, he lay prostrate and silent, flattened under the blankets. Once the trucks were gone and we were out for a walk, he would slink past the garbage cans, some of them still rolling in the street. And he would bark at them sharply. Ben, the garbage warrior.

I returned to Scotland for the month of August. A graduate student from Tufts, another David, stayed in the JP house with Ben and walked him four hours a day on the leash. His epic walks were designed to wear Ben out, and they did. Eventually Ben would lie quietly on a park bench in the Arboretum, his head resting on David's lap. Sometimes they waited for the sun to set. Those moments on the park bench were perfect, he told me. And it only took four hours to achieve that state of contentment.

But even David, whose tolerance for doggy behavior seemed infinite, had to admit that Ben was a little bit crazy. Not, however, crazy enough to keep him from getting his own Border Collie, Christie, with her own dear handicaps; but that's another story.

We returned to Boston at the beginning of September, a month that had always been complicated by back-to-school worries. But this month was different for everybody, for this was the September of 2001 when the fortresses came tumbling down. This was the Fall when we all hid under the bed and looked for terrorists in the most innocent places.

Ben still fought his own demons, the noises filling the air, the terrors on wheels rolling down the street, but for once he wasn't entirely alone. Dog walkers in the Arboretum shared theories about the ways that their animals had been traumatized, filled up to bursting with their owner's fears. September 11th began to explain the most eccentric canine behaviors.

"They're more sensitive than we are," the lovely owner of the terrible corgis explained. "They know so much more than we do. That's why they're so unruly just now; they just can't help themselves."

If it were only that simple, I thought, bracing myself for one more scramble through the bush after runaway Ben.

One afternoon, David was walking Ben on top of Hemlock Hill, off leash. Ben had been sniffing and capering, running up and down the rocks, when suddenly, he charged, straight down the steep precipice onto the road that led to Peter's Hill. David spent an hour running back and forth, down the mountain, crossing the street into Peter's Hill, up and down, crossing streets and walkways. Finally, beaten, he returned home where Ben was waiting in the back yard, nonplussed, tied to the porch rail. A dog walker had found him in the street and drove him to our house.

When David called to thank her, she responded rather tersely, but with sympathy, suggesting that Ben needed training. "You need to do something," she said, "about that dog. For his own good."

Not to mention our good. We couldn't even ask ourselves anymore why we were driving ourselves crazy. We loved each other, didn't we? Here we were with a second chance to make a life together, one that would include the kids, one that would open out into happiness and freedom, if we just were able to let go of Ben. But we were hanging on, filled with a dread impossible to shake.

Ben became so frightened that he started to refuse to leave the house. The sound of keys rattling in the bowl in the hall used to be a signal for him to race down the stairs looking for a walk. Now the sound of keys sent him under the bed. To get Ben downstairs, David resorted to ringing the doorbell. Avon calling. While Ben stood eagerly in front of the door waiting for it to open, I would snap on his leash and hold on tight, yank him down the front steps and force march him at least up to the end of the block.

Worse still, he didn't want us to leave him. We were fellow prisoners struggling to keep him safe. He started to stand rigidly, determined to block our approach to the front door. Then he would growl, bark, and finally throw himself at us if we dared to turn the doorknob. It became easier for me to sneak off to school, pretending to head towards the front door, only to turn suddenly and barrel out the back, sometimes making it down to the fence before Ben caught on.

Once he got wise, he began to obsess about my brief case. He knew that when it moved, I'd be following it out of the house and into the car to drive away from him. He guarded that case for dear life, snarling if I came near it. I tried crating him on my way to school, even if David was upstairs at the computer, but he began snapping at me when I tried getting him through the crate door. Sometimes David would call him upstairs, using the foolproof high pitched voice, "come sweet boy, come on you little nut," and sometimes he left the brief case behind and bounded up to David's study. And sometimes he didn't. I never exactly missed getting to school on time, but I frequently arrived disheveled and discomposed, my mind on Ben instead of Ned Ward's *London Spy*.

All the craziness began to fill me with shame. All the plans I had concocted to create the perfect dog mocked me. I stopped telling Ben stories. They had become too painful to spin.

So we entered one more round of training. Another behaviorist, perky, grandmotherly, spoke to us in high ringing sounds of encouragement and confidence. She came to our house to teach us clicker training—well designed for our dog's obsessive nature. Ben loved clicker training. As long as he stayed in the house, he could sit, lie down, and stay for hours, responding with great delight to the clicks that rewarded him for his compliance. Ears perked up, tail waving, grinning with anticipation at the very sight of the modest instrument, he was happy then.

But we still couldn't get him outside for very long and, if we did manage to get him down the front steps, he'd go immediately into slink mode, almost crawling down the street, belly pressed to the pavement. He looked beaten into submission by heartless owners.

I learned many new things from the new behaviorist. Most importantly, I was boring Ben to death. Where was the excitement, the energy to rouse him from his self-absorption? I was too calm, too placid, and too soothing. This piece of criticism certainly roused me.

"What do you mean?" I asked. I had been told repeatedly by the breeder and the trainers and the behaviorists that I needed to tone down my overly enthusiastic nature. I needed to settle, Carol, settle.

But now it seemed that I did too good a job settling. Now I was to speak to Ben in a high, jaunty voice and never give him sympathy.

When the garbage truck made its appointed round, terrorizing the neighborhood, I was never supposed to stroke Ben and tell him that it was going to be okay. No, I was to leap out of bed, and say in a funny voice, "don't be so silly, silly dog, come on now, we'll have a nice walk, come on, let's get that ball, don't be such a screwball." I needed to design a perkier model of my old enthusiastic self. Debbie Reynolds on speed. Somewhere along the line, I realized, I'd lost whatever character I had ever possessed.

Animals make you confront your real self. You know the one I mean— the clumsy one trying so hard to soar. The awkward one frozen in place. I knew that somewhere there could be a better me, strong and full of grace, but I kept on failing.

And the animals can smell failure. Sensing weakness, they will keep on nipping and grunting and growing, refusing to believe our stories that, deep down, humans are loving, helpful and good. Maybe they know all along that one day we will give up trying. Maybe that's why they make us question what we are doing for the love of them, as if love didn't come with a price.

I imagined for too long that if I kept working hard, the animals would love each other and us, creating our peaceable kingdom.

I believed that if our animals could love us that would mean that we would be loveable.

Perhaps I shouldn't use the plural here. *I* was the one who imagined these impossible things. Just as I believed that, if I worked very hard, I could make our "blended" family love each other and, of course, love me.

If I made enough stuffed potatoes and made enough trips to Franklin Park Zoo with Caitlin, if I stood with her for thirty minutes watching the aged lions sleeping, would that make her love me?

If David made enough crepes with lemon and sugar topping, would his children, and mine, and their children, into perpetuity, love him forever for his sweetness, for his tartness, for his dependable comfort?

What happens when these offerings to the domestic gods don't work? When love fails? And why shouldn't it fail? What makes us so special anyway?

Ben made us ask those questions, and provided no answers. But he did force us to see, partly, what we had to do about him.

We finally learned how to make ourselves understand that it had all become too hard. Poor Ben had been snapping and nipping at me, and barking furiously in my face when I came near him with the leash. Walks lasted five minutes. Molly was refusing to visit after Ben managed to climb out of the crate, our Houdini. He appeared miraculously downstairs, right under our noses, to prance around Caitlin.

We tried to laugh, but the behaviorist worried that Ben would turn on me. If he did, she warned, the attack could be worse than the last time. Such skepticism coming from our professionally upbeat specialist, no cheery high voice here, but deep and serious tones of foreboding, made us finally take action.

We called Jennifer in the middle of December and arranged to board Ben. When we told her about Ben's meltdown, she said that she would think about keeping him. And we knew, talking to her, that we would probably never see Ben again because we could not keep failing him and ourselves.

Over the next two days, we took a roll of photographs. As long as he didn't have to leave the house, Ben became positively photogenic. He grinned at the camera, cocking his head, he sat still with a ball stuck firmly in his shiny teeth, he hid behind the door, his tail waving behind him, and he slept on his back, spread across the sofa, feet wiggling in the air.

David packed up every ball, chew toy, blanket, the comb, the nail clippers, the brush, the bowl, the leashes, the collars, the bags of kibble, the heartworm medication, the special shampoo, and the clickers, and then he broke down the crate and stuffed its components into its cardboard box.

Ben and I watched him carry these doggy idols out to the car and I snapped one more picture of him, the last on the roll. Ben jumped up on me as I was depressing the shutter. He shoved me so hard that he knocked the camera right out of my hands. It fell to the floor and cracked wide open.

And that was the end of thirty-six shots of Ben dancing, Ben prancing, probably the last one showed Ben crashing into the camera flying into air, thirty six shots exposed to the light.

David put the leash on Ben one last time, crying, and David never cries. He walked slowly down the stairs, pulling gently on the leash, and made his way to the car, and carefully let Ben into the back seat and shut the door. Then he walked back into the house.

"This has to be the end, you know, I can't really stand any more of this; it's too hard," he said, quickly, and he held me. When he stopped crying, he returned to the car and drove away, Ben barking his high-pitched crazy bark all the way down the street.

Ben boarded with Jennifer, but she didn't want to encourage us. She noticed the same weird behaviors that we had seen, the funny look he would get in his eyes just before he bolted. He was charging across three acres fenced in, running all the way to the farthest corner of the property, racing into the barn to hide in the straw, hiding in the house behind the sofa. He never snapped at her, but then what dog would?

But even Jennifer was starting to doubt her power over such a nutty collie. She was giving him bike rides, ten miles a day, attaching him to an exercise device that I can only imagine, and she assigned him jobs to do around the kennel. He took care, she said, of the little dogs when he wasn't being squirrelly or spooked.

Three of her friends, all dog trainers, spent an afternoon with Ben, and they used the word "manic" to describe him. I started calling Border Collie Rescue Leagues. One sympathetic link in the dispatch system told me that I knew what I had to do.

"Nobody is going to take that dog," she said, not after all of his aggressive behavior. "Not after it's been documented." And then she cleared her throat and whispered, "You know what you need to do."

But we knew that we couldn't put Ben down, and we knew now that we couldn't bring him home. We could pay Jennifer twenty dollars a day. What would that be yearly? Just a little over seven thousand dollars, the price of tuition to a minor university or college. A college that could not teach us how to do what we knew that we needed to do. It was a bargain, really, turning Ben over to a foster parent better qualified to care for him.

"Where's Ben," friends wanted to know. "Where's Ben," dog walkers in the Arboretum asked, and sometimes we would tell the terrible story over and over like ancient mariners. And sometimes we silently hurried away, covered in shame.

And then, in March, Jennifer called. "I'll keep him," she said. "He's a nut, but you know, he's such a funny little guy. And he likes the horses."

I won't try to describe how silent the house seemed without Ben and how we wandered, ghost-like, up and down the stairs and out into the back yard looking for signs—a water-logged tennis ball, a buried bone, a turd hiding in the bamboo, a wisp of black hair attached to the current bush.

But I can say that I was never able to wash his paw prints and the signs of his doggy drool from the front porch windows overlooking the Saab.

My First Dog

I HADN'T THOUGHT ABOUT DORA for years. It was only after Ben, not just the experience of Ben, but in writing about Ben, that I found the memory of Dora, so startlingly intact. She brought me back to my mother and those early days in Chicago, and she made me remember my mother's anger and how it drove me out of the house and into the garage. Dora saved me, for at least two weeks, by giving me a furry, springy, uncomplicated body to hold onto and a place where I could feel safe. My mother seemed hard and unforgiving; Dora seemed soft and generous, open to my need to be touched and loved.

Can it be that simple, the animal hunger that comes from the fundamental need to fill the hole in the heart? The collateral damage that follows such dangerous emotional transplants shouldn't be surprising. But still, even now, even after the damage has been done, I am astonished by the extent of my greed for the warmth and comfort that an animal promises—or seems to promise—to provide. Coming to the end of the histories of the animals, putting to rest the last tale of the last dog, I find myself at the very beginning of that animal itch. And in the beginning, my beginning, was Dora.

My second-cousin-once-removed John and I found Dora shivering in her sleep, pressed against the trashcan next to the Hills' garage. She was a little dog, long and low, sort of a cross between a beagle and a dachshund, but her spotted coat—black and brown and white—was shaggy and long, snarled and very dirty. *Filthy*, my mother would have said, if, that is, she could have seen her. Not that she would ever lay her eyes on my dog.

And this was definitely My Dog. No collar. Nobody to claim her. She was My Dog from the start.

We'd been throwing our Spauldeens against our garage door when we first saw her. That's what we usually did in the alley, that or play Demetrius and the Gladiators. This particular November afternoon was too cold to run around in velvet cloaks and togas made out of sheets. Better to slam a pink rubber ball against a wooden door hard enough to make it shake.

The alley separated my block, Church Street, from John's block, Hermosa. It was almost always empty during the day, waiting for the fathers to roll into their garages at 5:30 or maybe 6 at night. The mothers didn't own cars then; that came later, around 1957.

The alley was the neighborhood male preserve, where the fathers fiddled around on the weekends. They sat on stools or boxes, or leaned against the wall, each father snug in his own garage, only occasionally visiting each other's domain, smoking (my dad liked Panatelas), listening to the game—there was always a game—on their portable radios.

They listened while they cleaned their tools, lining up their rakes and their brooms. Sometimes they leafed furtively through lurid magazines hidden inside stacks of Popular Mechanics and Field and Stream. We knew because we watched them through the garage windows.

It was 1955 and I was ten years old, halfway through my decade of allergies. I was allergic to mold, dust, grass, kapok, willows, roses, cats, birds, wool, flour, horses, dandelions, ragweed, and, of course, dogs. Shots, three times a week, were supposed to protect me from what my doctor called my allergic tendencies. My tendencies occasionally erupted into asthma attacks that provoked frantic trips to the emergency room where I was given shots of adrenaline that made me shiver and shake and talk too fast.

That's how I knew that we needed to keep Dora a secret. Dogs, cats, rabbits and hamsters were forbidden. I could only keep dumb pets like goldfish and turtles, cold and slimy creatures incapable of affection that inevitably died from over feeding.

Dora, I could tell, had not been fed in a long while. She was that skinny. We would have to keep her to save her. Since John already had a dog, an overweight lassie type named Lassie, drooling, smelly, getting senile, he knew that he couldn't bring home another dog, no matter how needy.

"She's starving," I insisted. "Look at her ribs sticking out."

By now we had roused the puppy. She was wriggling her hairy, bony body, hugging my legs, shaking with excitement. "She loves me," I cried. "She's probably just hungry," John said in his stoic way, practicing to be John Wayne. Still, he loped home to bring back some kibble and a bowl of milk, the first of many raids he would make for Dora and me.

I wonder now at his patient tolerance. Then, I just took it for granted. When I ran into him at a family funeral a few years ago, I asked him why he had been so kind to me those the doggy days in the alley.

"What dog?" he asked. "You never had a dog; you were allergic. What are you talking about?" When I insisted upon my story, he suggested that I was confusing him with somebody else on Hermosa, Rory O'Shea, maybe, or one of the Sheehan kids.

"No way I could ever forget a dog named Dora," he said. "Dora? What a weird name for a dog."

I called her Dora because she was adorable. "I didn't know about Freud then," I said, laughing. John just stared at me. "You always did like to make things up," he said, squinting hard. "I remember that about you all right."

Did I ever really have Dora, even for two weeks? Yes. Absolutely. John just forgot.

Waiting for John, I kept Dora warm under my jacket. I could feel her cold, leathery nose rooting around under my arm, her tongue licking my neck. "She probably has fleas," John had warned, his parting words, but I didn't mind. I stretched out against the garage door to feel her scrabbling around my stomach and chest.

I dragged a plywood box that had once held Indian River grapefruits out from the basement. We lined the box with newspapers, a moth-eaten, hand-knit sweater from John's mother's ragbag and a couple of beach towels I found in the bottom of the linen closet. Dora lived in the box in my garage, hidden in the corner behind the piles of old newspapers that were waiting for the next Boy Scout drive. Too little to climb out, she seemed content enough to curl into a ball waiting for us to come and play.

We were able to sneak in and out of the garage with relative ease once we perfected our diversionary strategy. While John carefully opened the garage door, I threw my Spauldeen against the side, making as much noise as possible.

I practiced walking in backwards, as if I were walking out, until John reminded me that I would still be connected to the garage, coming or going.

"Not good," he said. "You got to think like a spy."

We would dash in quickly, and I would freeze against the wall while John smoothly let down the door. "Quiet door," he noticed with approval, "your dad must keep it well oiled."

We managed to walk Dora in the morning, before school, at noon after watching "Uncle Johnny Coons' Lunch Time Little Theatre," and again in the afternoon when we raced home from school to get to the alley before the other kids on our blocks. My asthma dependably kicked in a block or so before we got to the alley. John would always run ahead to open the garage door, waiting for me to catch my breath.

I can still see him smiling there, holding Dora. She'd leap out of his arms into mine, licking my face hard, nipping me softly on the ear. Once we tied Dora's leash, an old clothesline I stole from the basement, around her neck, I'd stuff her wriggling under my coat until we reached Prospect, the street two blocks from the alley. Walking Dora down Church or Hermosa would be too dangerous, we thought; she would be noticed, and we would be questioned. It was easier to walk Dora at night. After dark, none of us kids were out and about, but then, that also presented a problem.

I didn't have any particular place to go in the pitch dark at 8 p.m. John came by instead, walking an unsuspecting and often confused Lassie, who sometimes snapped at Dora for getting in her way.

It's a wonder that my father didn't catch on, but then he always tore into and out of the garage. Mornings he was determined to beat the traffic, evenings he'd be exhausted from the day and ready for a Manhattan. He never noticed the furry creature trying to jump out of her box, but then my father was never very observant. He preferred not to look very hard around the house, spending his energy on the White Sox and the Bears or on the blueprints and plans that he brought home each night from work. Besides, Dora was remarkably quiet. She only barked when we called out her name.

Saturday was tricky. That was the day that dad puttered about in the garage, even in the coldest days of November. Saturdays John smuggled Dora out early in the morning, walked her up and down Prospect, and managed to sneak her into his room, where she spent the day curled up on his bed. After breakfast, I followed, spending the morning doing math homework on his bedroom floor. My real incompetence at math made this ploy quite convincing. Besides, John's mother liked me because I had good manners. Please, thank you, excuse me; may I help you, may I?

We never worried about fooling my mother. In spite of the fact that she always bragged about having eyes in the back of her head, she was too preoccupied with the mysteries of the household to keep her eye on the garage. She scrubbed the kitchen floor tiles, banging the scrub brush against the cabinets, she scoured the bathroom sink and bowl, wiped clean the glass droplets on the chandelier, shaking them until they sang, and she dusted with careful deliberation the Hummel figures lining the mantle piece.

Every Monday, down in the basement, she presided over the laundry, that inner sanctum full of fumes and steam and anger, threatening to put my hair into the wringer and pull it out by the roots if I didn't behave. And every week she produced one boiled smoked butt, pans of pigs in blankets, gallons of stuffed green peppers, vats of chicken a la king, and quivering mountains of green and yellow Jell-O surprises. She had a real talent for baking, and faithfully produced either a pie or cake for every dinner, sometimes a la mode. Plum Pie was her specialty.

The Angel in the House, she worked like a demon, washing and ironing and cleaning and cooking and baking. Anything not inside the house remained permanently outside of her range of vision. Outside is where she drove my brother and me to play, jabbing us with her broom, her mop, her finger to get us the hell out of her way. The garage might have been located on a distant planet in another galaxy as far as she was concerned. She did wonder where the clothesline had gone. I told her that I needed it for a project on sailing vessels in the Revolutionary War.

It's amazing to remember how much freedom we had then. Here we were, living on the south side of Chicago, too close to the railroad tracks, wandering at will up and down the alleys, and in and out of each other's houses. We set campfires in vacant lots where we roasted potatoes, we broke into boarded up haunted houses, climbed trees as high as we could manage, and sailed off each other's back porch railings to prove our bravery.

Once I jumped off Chuckie Nash's garage roof, wrapped in a toga, holding an umbrella. We rode our bicycles as far as they would take us—in my case not that far, because I usually started wheezing after seven or eight blocks and had to walk back to my house by myself.

Playing meant leaving the house after we had done our homework (half an hour at the max) and not getting back until it got dark. We were of course under a certain degree of surveillance. All of those mothers who stayed home, cleaning and cooking, tried to keep an eye on us.

But we managed to get away with a lot. I used to run away on a regular basis, meeting new neighbors on distant blocks who sat on their front porches playing canasta and drinking iced tea.

Running away got me out of the house and out of my mother's reach.

"She's on a rampage," my dad would warn. "You'd better run for it, lie low, get the hell out of her way. You know she's got a short fuse, a low boiling point, she's a real pistol."

His clichéd jokes failed to disguise the urgency of her anger. Not that he ever knew her down in the basement where she sometimes hit me hard, to make me—so grimy and insubordinate—cleaner and better. He could warn me to lie low, but he could never make me safe.

That's why the garage was such an attractive hideout those cold November days. Wrapped up in old blankets, I could whisper endearments to the snuggly puppy, washed clean one sunny day, rubbed to a high gleam by John, who had borrowed Lassie's brush. Not just lying low, I curled around Dora who was keeping me warm, keeping me safe from harm.

We did worry about keeping Dora amused. She was lonely, we imagined, stuck in the dark and drafty garage. She needed to be entertained. John brought his tiny transistor radio, turned it down low, and tucked it into the wooden box. After deciding that Dora liked to hear Latin music, I pretended to rumba with her as she struggled to stay up on her two back legs. She wobbled to the strains of Xavier Cugat. I checked out a book on dog training from the Walker branch library.

"Roll over," I whispered, "play dead." Dora only looked at me, brown eyes soft, opening wide in confusion.

"Lick my hand," I commanded. That she could do. And I would hug her hard against me, breathing in her dog smell, rubbing my nose into her fluffy, scruffy coat and trying not to break out in eczema or begin to wheeze.

These were the happiest of days. Dora was the most beautiful, intelligent, the funniest and most responsive dog in the whole world. In truth, she was a little loopy looking. Her lower jaw jutted out. "She needs braces," John said, but I ignored him, and saw beneath Dora's under bite an animal of exceptional quality, the future winner of the annual Morgan Park dog show. "And a rabies shot," he would add, "and a dog license. I'm not kidding. And where are we gonna get the money? Don't look at me."

We worried most about staying invisible. Dora needed to be a secret kept from everybody. Twenty-seven other kids lived on our blocks, most of them with big mouths. If I told Jean, she would tell Laurie, and Laurie would tell her mother and her mother would turn us in to my mother. We couldn't breathe a word to any living soul about Dora, no matter how much our friends pestered.

In spite of our attempts to disguise our preoccupation, it had been observed that we were spending far too much time hiding in the garage when we should have been playing kick the can and capture the flag.

"What are you guys doing in there?" Bobby wanted to know. Bobby lived next door. I felt bad not telling Bobby; he was my best friend, but his dad, Kas, was a cop. He'd get it out of his son in no time at all. Just like in Dragnet. Kas always had his eye on us ever since we almost burned the telephone wires. Bobby and I had discovered the summer before that if you spit or squirt water into boiling wax, you can produce flames one or two feet tall. Encouraged by our experiments, we each threw a cup of water into the bubbling cauldron of melted candles. That's when we scorched the wires twelve feet up in the air. Unfortunately, Kas was looking out the kitchen window.

"I've got you in my book," he warned. "Don't even think about getting out of line."

Jean was the most relentless inquisitor. She knew what we were doing in the garage. K-i-s-s-i-n-g.

"Oh yuk," I answered disdainfully. "Oh yuk yuk yuk y-u-k." I don't think about John that way. I don't think about anybody that way; you're gross."

Once I saw her little head bobbing outside the garage window. I recognized her blue tasseled hat. She was probably jumping up and down trying to peek in to catch us in the act. Luckily, the window was so grimy that she wouldn't have been able to see into the dark corner where Dora was doing the rumba. But we knew that she was getting too close to our secret.

We also worried about the weather. It was almost Thanksgiving. The sky was getting that dull, steely gray color that promised snow any day. We made ourselves march around to keep our feet from freezing, and I thought about making Dora a doggy jacket.

"You can't sew," John reminded.

"I can learn," I answered half-heartedly, but I knew that he was right.

Food became the biggest problem. At first, it didn't seem difficult for John to smuggle a few handfuls of kibble out of Lassie's enormous supply, but of course Dora was getting a little bigger. How big would she get, we wondered. How much more would she need to eat? Was she a cross between a Beagle and a St. Bernard? We'd need to get jobs to pay for the bags of kibble, the gallons of milk. What if she got sick?

"More likely," John said, "we'll get sick freezing to death in the garage." He was losing interest, he warned me, and besides he already had a dog.

"A stupid senile dog," I said, "and she doesn't know how to rumba."

"Stop whispering so loudly," he answered; "we're going to get caught."

Mrs. Jorgenson finally turned us in. She lived kitty corner from us across the alley, and gave me allergy shots three times a week. Before she got married, she'd been a nurse at Little Company of Mary even though she was Swedish Lutheran. I liked her well enough; she didn't hurt too much and usually she gave me a gingersnap after the shots.

I sat in her kitchen as usual, waiting for the first jab, closing my eyes, when I heard her say quite severely, in her sing song way, "Carol Louise, open your eyes and look at me."

I did.

"Now," she said, "your asthma, it's worse, yah?" I shrugged, not wanting to answer. "And you know why your asthma is acting up?"

I shrugged again. That was a mistake. She leaned over and sniffed hard. "Because you smell of dog. You see this hypodermic." She pointed it at me. The needle glittered. "So here I am in my kitchen, and I am just about ready to fill the needle with this serum, yah, this serum that is supposed to protect you from dog dander. Three times a week I do this for you, and meanwhile you are hiding in the garage with a shaggy, dirty dog, rolling around with her, covering yourself with her dander, you and that John. You see, I can watch you from my back yard, when I hang up the laundry. I saw that Jeanie jump up and down trying to see into the window. At first I don't know what to think. You are not old enough to be doing anything bad in the garage. Even you couldn't be that bad, yah?"

She laughed then. *Oh boy,* I thought, *this is not good.*

"So Jeanie, such a nosy little girl, she finally goes home, and then I see you sneak out like silly spies in a movie, you and that John, so I walk across the alley, and open the garage door. And there it is, the little dog, like a jack in the box, wagging her tail, ready to play. Why not get yourself a cat while you're at it? See this vial of serum; this is for the cat dander. Next you could get yourself a horse, or a parrot maybe. Why don't you rub grass cuttings all over you, good for your eczema? Why not? Give me your arm, you silly girl."

She made the shots hurt. No gingersnaps followed, just more talk about how I had to tell my mother all about the dog.

"Her name is Dora," I said. Mrs. Jorgenson made a sucking noise with her lips. "Dora, Snora, she's not your dog. She makes you sick."

I said nothing at first, practicing John practicing John Wayne. I wouldn't let Mrs. Jorgenson get in my way. *No ma'am.* So after giving her my most inscrutable look, I thanked her kindly, ma'am, and ran out of her kitchen, down the steps, past the clothes line, straight into the garage; I didn't care if she saw me.

Dora seemed to wave from her box, faithful, funny, bobbing up and down a little like Jeanie in her silly hat. I picked her up, held her to me, and thought: We could run away together, really run away. I would need to steal some money from my mother's envelopes. She kept them in her top dresser drawer. Some of the envelopes were for paying bills, the gas, the lights, the real estate tax, food and donations to the church. I couldn't take money from there; she'd notice.

But she had another envelope, hidden under her stockings, full of what she called her "mad money," dollar bills that she saved from the food envelope to spend on coats and dresses for me, the ungrateful one, and for her. Then she'd tell my father that the clothes were marked down. "On sale," she used to announce in triumph, her eyes shining. She would show him the price tag that she had altered herself in black ink.

"See," she'd say, "marked down fifty percent."

She always looked her prettiest in those moments after hours of shopping at Goldblatts and Wieboldts, and sometimes Carson Pirie

Scott, stimulated by her minor acts of embezzlement. Her envelope helped pay for the violet coat I had worn last April to Easter service at St John the Divine. That was the envelope to steal from, the one full of her mad money. Besides, she wouldn't need to buy me any more coats.

Dora licked my nose and barked. She was getting bored. What about the rumba? she seemed to be asking. What about the commands? Dead Dog, Roll Over, Speak. She barked again, not listening to me whispering and shushing to keep her quiet.

I held her for a long time, even after she wriggled hard enough to make me stop. Then she nipped me with her baby teeth sharp as needles. I started to imagine what it would be like to get rabies. Foaming at the mouth. Great thirst. I could bite Mrs. Jorgenson.

"Mrs. Jorgenson is right," I told Dora. "You need a real home with real kids who take you for real walks and make you roll over, be dead and speak. But you're still mine. You'll always be mine."

It would be hard to get a job, I thought. It wasn't as if I could even baby-sit. I was too young and pulling weeds did not seem to be a terribly profitable occupation. Not in November. I couldn't ask John to run away with me. That would be going too far. He had done enough. We weren't even good enough friends. Now Bobby—Bobby would, but no, his dad would pick us up before we got to the end of the block.

But what if I showed up at the railroad station, not that far away, only three blocks, carrying Dora under my coat, and what if I bought a train ticket from Morgan Park to the big station in the Loop? And what if once I got there, what if I just sort of stood around the ticket counter, looking a little worried, furrowing my brow. Not looking worried enough to arouse suspicion, not looking frantic, you understand, until I finally found a kindly old gentleman with enormous white mustaches who turned out to be my long-lost grandfather.

That's because I had been adopted. My real parents had been killed in a fiery crash in the Alps. They had been driving madly home from a fancy party, took a turn too quickly, and fell to their deaths. Somehow, I got lost in the shuffle, never discovered until now. It was the butler's fault; he'd been drinking.

I could see it now, clearly. My maternal grandfather, the Earl of Sausage, would gaze at me in astonishment and he would say, tearfully, "You are the living image of my daughter, Eleanor Ramona; you must be my long lost grandchild. Come to me, my dear child. I will make you my heir and shower you with diamonds and rubies and as much vanilla ice cream with Hershey's chocolate syrup as you can eat."

And then I would reach under my coat to produce Dora and say, "Only if you will take this beloved dog, her name is Dora. We must never be separated."

We could do it, I thought. I would just have to wash my hair and let my mother put it into curls, and I would need to wear that really sickening alpine looking Heidi dress that we bought on sale, really on sale. Nobody would buy that one full price.

I thought these things and pondered them in my heart. That was from my line in the Christmas pageant. I would need to miss the pageant this year, but I would never forget my line: *But Mary kept all these things, and pondered them in her heart.*

For one lousy line, I had to go to rehearsal every Thursday night. But it was a good line, and I realized that I was no less preoccupied with my miraculous puppy than Mary was when she worried about the baby Jesus. Would it be blasphemous to think of the garage as a sort of stable? Probably. I sighed. Meanwhile, I could hear Mrs. Jorgenson outside the garage. She was knocking on the window, and saying quite loudly, "Carol Louise, I am giving you two minutes to come out of there."

I burrowed down into Dora, and kept quiet. They would have to drag me out of the garage. And I would not leave without making a big ruckus. When I wasn't being polite, I was famous for making big ruckuses, which is probably why my mother was frequently on a rampage banging me against the wall. Or was it vice versa?

I didn't care then to ponder these thoughts in my heart or anywhere else. I just wanted to run away, but I knew that Mrs. Jorgenson would cut me off at the pass. It figured. What sort of woman offers, voluntarily, to give kids shots, accepting no pay? Mrs. Jorgenson had to be harboring sadistic tendencies. Her heart was black.

Nobody came out to drag me from the garage. I was there for about three hours, from three-fifteen—the time when I went over as usual to Mrs. Jorgenson's—until six fifteen, when my father pulled up in the Chevy, opened and shut the car door, loudly, and walked over to the garage door.

"Carol Louise," he shouted. "Your mother called me at work. Come out this instant."

I rolled over into a fetal position, shoving Dora under my jacket, and placed my finger into her sharp baby mouth to keep her from gnawing on my stomach. I closed my eyes and waited. And waited. I could hear my dad start up the Chevy. He drove off.

Nobody else came to the garage door. It got boring. I got hungry. And I realized that Dora needed a walk. Poor John. I hoped that he wouldn't walk into this mess. They would be all over him and it wasn't his fault.

It was finally Dora who drove me out of the garage. She was such a wonderfully house-trained—make that garage-trained—dog, but even she had her limits. Who taught her how to hold it until she could leave the garage and go on her walks? Maybe she did have an owner after all. Maybe her collar had fallen off like John said.

I opened the garage door, the well-oiled door that flew up into the rafters as if by magic. Nobody was there. It was dark in the alley, no stars, no moon, not one car in sight and no kids, not even Jean. But across the yard, the little bungalow lit up the sky, every electric bulb blazing. After I let Dora pee in the alley, I carried her into the yard, walked warily up the cement path past the dead Irises, and found my brother wrapped in a blanket, sitting on the back porch, waiting for me. He was only six, but he knew.

"You're in big trouble," he said, "don't do anything stupid."

Stupid head, stupid head, stupid head, I yelled at myself as I moved through the eerily empty kitchen, the dining room, also empty, and opened the French doors into, oh no, the living room. Nobody ever sat in the living room, except on Christmas Eve or Easter Morning. But they were all there. Mom and Dad, Kas, John's mother, Mrs. Jorgenson and two grown-ups I didn't know. They were holding onto a little girl's hands. She was pale and fat and had light brown hair, and she was crying loudly, with feeling. What a jerk, I thought. Nobody sobs like that for real.

My mother grabbed me by my arm, squeezing it tightly, and tugging on my hair, hard, she threw me into the big chair with the duck print seat covers.

"It's time we talked, young lady," I heard her say, but I began to tune her out. I didn't even hear the young lady part. I knew that it was there, because she ended just about every sentence that way.

It's time for bed, young lady, time to brush the snarls out of your hair, young lady, and time to get off your high horse, young lady.

Mrs. Jorgenson sniffed loudly, giving her nose a loud blow before she began.

"So," she said, "so, I am leaving my house to walk up and down the street to think about the problem of the little dog, that's the one that is bouncing up and down inside Carol's coat, you know, and I saw suddenly on the lamp posts signs, made of paper, with a picture of the unfortunately ugly dog on them, and the words, Lost. Reward. Call this number. And I did, and here are the owners, the Randolphs and their lovely daughter Corrine, who have been searching for Mitzi for over two weeks now. They have suffered, yah, while you are romping around with the unfortunate dog in the garage. They live down your street, Carol Louise, in the apartments."

In the apartments, I thought, raising a dog like Dora in those dreadfully tiny rooms. We never even trick or treated over there. No wonder Dora was happy enough to live in a box. The apartments! No back yards. No alley.

Corrine looked at me with little piggy eyes. I didn't know her because she went to Lutheran school. (I found that out later, when we became friends and played canasta in the afternoons, teaching Dora how to do the two-step.)

"I will always hate you," she said, "for the rest of my life. You stole my dog."

"Where's your proof," I sneered. "Where's her collar? I don't see her wagging her tail at you. She's my dog, mine."

"Carol Louise," said Mrs. Jorgenson, "bring that ugly dog out from under your jacket and maybe, just maybe, she will have a chance to wag her anything whatsoever."

She thought that she was so funny. I vowed never to let her give me another shot.

I held onto Dora for one last time, let her nip my fingers, and pulled her slowly out from under my sweater.

"She's not ugly," I yelled.

Dora looked up at me, started to whine, and ran into the dreadful Corrine's arms.

"My Mitzi, my Mitzi," I heard her crying.

I wanted to throw up. I was definitely not going to have an asthma attack. I decided to look at my feet instead. I prepared a speech about how I would say nothing, and how I would not apologize, but there was no need.

The Randolph family marched out of the house through the front door, the one on the side of our house that faced Bobby's front door across the gangway. I could see half of his face pressed against the diamond shaped front door window, watching, waiting and trying to stay out of Kas's way. He waved at me, his hand fluttering past the other window.

I endured, of course, weeks of punishments, corporal, spiritual, intellectual, but they didn't matter. I had lost Dora, my dog, and, believe me, teaching Mitzi the two step, and dressing her up in a clown suit when the dog wasn't my dog, and when the friend was not really a friend, more like a pain, could not make up for the vacant spot in the corner of the garage, in the corner of my heart.

BEN AGAIN

I ASKED YOU TO TRUST ME. I assured you that Ben is safe in New Hampshire with Jennifer and the horses. But that is a lie. It wasn't a lie when I first wrote about Ben's good fortune, settling into life on Jennifer's farm in New Hampshire. But when I was revising that chapter, I learned that things had changed.

I tried to rewrite Ben's fate, but just couldn't erase that small but invaluable space of happiness that seemed to open up, the hope for Ben settling in. Settling. I'd still lie if I had to do it over. It was worth it, to keep, for a little longer, the illusion of Ben coming to a place of peace.

The truth is I don't know where he is. About a year after we gave Ben to Jennifer, I saw Ted, Jennifer's husband, standing outside of JP Licks.

"Ted," I said, "Ted, how are you, and how's Ben?"

Ted looked puzzled. He didn't seem to know who I was.

"How's Ben," he said, "Ben?"

And then he smiled. Ted is a large and gentle man. He used to tell me that when Ben ran wild, when Jennifer couldn't take it any more, that Ben would come running up to him and hug his legs for comfort.

"Ben," he said. "Of course; you're Ben's mother. You know, he's doing much better. He really likes it up in New Hampshire."

"But he already was in New Hampshire with you and Jennifer. Where's Ben now?"

Ted hesitated.

I waited.

"Well, you know how squirrelly he could get. That little guy was just too high strung. Jennifer was biking with him behind the bike ten, twelve miles a day. He got enough exercise, but he never really calmed down. He just never seemed to know how to get comfortable. But he's on a farm now, in northern New Hampshire. Where there's room to run wild."

"Can I call Jennifer?" I asked.

He smiled again. "Sure. I bet she'd love to hear from you. But you know, she'll tell you the same thing. That Ben's just a nutty little guy."

I did call Jennifer. And after she didn't call me back, I called two more times, leaving messages, and then I tried again, twice. By then I was scared. What would I learn?

I remembered Denny telling us about Dixie running free in Montana, or was it Idaho, and being adopted by dog lovers in Vermont. His stories always seemed bogus, but perhaps there really was a dog underground sending the truly incorrigible up the road to live free or die.

After a month or so, I tried to call Jennifer again. But her number had been changed. I learned that she moved back to Massachusetts because she had a 978 area code, but I still couldn't get her to call me back. I stopped trying. She's a good woman who made, I know, every effort she could for a dog who couldn't be helped. I didn't want to make things harder for her than Ben did.

But oh, how I wanted to crawl under the covers and wait for Ben to jump on top of my head. I wanted him to place his bony little paws on my shoulders. I even wanted to feel him squirm and shiver, waiting for the garbage truck to slither down the rainy Monday morning street, bracing himself for the back up noise, *beep, beep, beep.*

But I also knew that I was lying to myself. I really wanted Ben, running free, not hiding under the bed, terrified in JP. Maybe he did end up somewhere in New Hampshire, or is it Montana, or Vermont, with all the lost dogs, all the ones who can never come home again. Maybe he met up with Dixie; maybe they dance together under the stars. But he can't be dead. Oh no. Not Ben. Ben could never die.

One night, asleep in our bed, asleep without Ben between us, David started talking in his sleep. There was nothing unusual in that. David plays rugby in his sleep, sings in his sleep and even laughs in his sleep. Talking is a relatively mild behavior for him, far preferable to mistaking me for an opponent that he needs to push out of bed.

There was a full moon that night and light was pouring into the window bleaching him whiter than the sheets. He looked young and vulnerable, and he lay still, not thrashing around at all. He was smiling.

David was talking, and this is what he said.

When oh when
Then
Then oh then
Oh When Oh
Ben
Ben
Ben
Hi Ben
Hi Ben
Hi Ben
Hi Ben

And so we sleep and dream. And sleep and dream again.

Once, Carol. Just say it once.

Settle.

Carol Houlihan Flynn grew up on the South Side of Chicago. She received her BA from the University of Illinois, an MA in American Civilization from Brown and a Ph.D. in English from U.C. Berkeley. She lived in London for four years where she worked in the British Library on Samuel Richardson, author of *Clarissa*. She also began writing fiction and worked with the Women's Research and Resources Centre on feminist approaches to literature.

When she returned to the United States, she taught eighteenth-century English Literature at NYU, Princeton and Tufts. She retired from Tufts in 2011 to write fiction and memoir.

Some of her published works include *Washed in the Blood*, a mystery novel set in 1938 Los Angeles (Putnam, 1983), *Samuel Richardson, A Man of Letters* (1982) and *The Body in Swift and Defoe* (2005).

She's just finishing her novel, *The Burnt Hills*, set in Berkeley, 1974.

Carol and her husband, David Tarbet, divide their time between Boston and Kirkcudbright in Southwest Scotland. She's pictured sitting on a hillside of heather in Scotland.

Lightning Source UK Ltd.
Milton Keynes UK
UKOW03f2015180514

231891UK00001B/1/P